W9-BUS-121

2nd Edition

Negotiate and Settle Your Debts

A Debt Settlement Strategy

By Mandy Akridge

JESSAMINE COUNTY PUBLIC LIBRARY
600 South Main Street
Nicholasville, KY 40356
(859) 885-3523

Contents

3 2530 60698 8994

DEC 1 5 2011

Copyright © 2009 by Mandy Akridge

Notice: Nothing in this book is intended to constitute legal advice. All sample forms are for educational purposes. If in doubt, please seek the advice of competent legal counsel. No warranties are made regarding the suitability of this book. This is an accumulation of information and not guaranteed. If you are not sure about the validity of something, please check elsewhere or get legal counsel.

All rights reserved. No part of this book may be reproduced by any means – without prior permission of the publisher.

Introduction

....

The reason for this came about when I found myself out of a job, and in the first time in twenty plus years, unable to find work. Never having been in this position before, it became apparent that we (as a nation) are coming into an age of a different time. Not wanting to believe we were truly in a recession here, I happily kept going along confidently, expecting to find work, but didn't. As the months went by, the credit card bills, mortgage, and everything else starting mounting up, whilst my bank accounts starting getting empty

As this started happening, I spent hundreds of hours researching debt, and debt settlement strategies. After accumulating a large amount of information, finally spent over a hundred dollars on a so-called guru's course, and much to my annoyance, it had exactly the same information that I had found and put together on my own. Showing my own success by using this strategy of debt settlement, this information has been put together in a format which would be easy to follow, and inexpensive enough for anyone to be able to obtain.

By June 2009, through two separate bills, Congress authorized the Treasury department to spend 1.1 trillion dollars of **taxpayer's money** to rescue the financial institutions. 700 billion dollars has been given to the banks to the tune of Bank of America 52.5 billion, Citigroup 50 billion, Wells Fargo 25 billion, PNC Financial Services 7.6 billion, not to mention AIG, General Motors, and the list goes on. Let's not forget the separate $400 billion reserved for Fannie Mae and Freddie Mac.

Now let's see what those banks have done to us (the people who've paid to bail them out). Miss one payment by a day and your interest rate can easily jump to almost 30%. Have high balances, they freeze your credit line and raise your interest rate to 30%. Perhaps your profile "resembles" someone who might default, once again, freeze or shut down your account with no warning, and raise your interest rate to 30%. Have a business credit line? That gets frozen too, even if you are dependent on it to keep your business going. ***Starting to see a pattern here?*** Then, the economy starts to crumble, and 700,000 people a month start to lose their jobs, and stop paying their credit cards, because their mortgage payment is more important.

So now, around 10% of people in the USA are unemployed. This is the highest in nearly 26 years as of 2010. The economy recession has caused the loss of six million jobs since the recession began in 2007. How many of those people have credit cards? Probably 99.9%. The banking industry by this stage should be getting nervous with everything from huge mortgage defaults to delinquent credit card debts. The national credit card debt is close to a trillion dollars. Hmm, seems to this author, the 1.1 trillion dollars could have been put to better use, but then, that's just an opinion. In any event, the new credit law only took effect in February 2010, so now, the banks get to no longer do exactly what they want as regards to rate hikes. Currently, now in January 2011, we are still in a very perilous situation as regards to the recession we are in. Not only individually are we facing financial crises, but even more so as a nation, being there are huge financial debts, such as the deficit which is on the way to reach 1.4 trillion dollars now in 2011.

A depression, such as the one in 1929, which lasted until the late 1930's, is just a worse form of a prolonged recession (which is not that far off from what we have been experiencing). The recovery from that depression was slow back then. This recession has been continuing quite strongly since 2008 starting with the housing bubble back in 2006, also with a very slow recovery. Unemployment, as mentioned above, which is close to 30 million people here in the USA, has not significantly improved. In fact, the real unemployment number is around 18.5 percent according to recent studies which include people who lost high paying jobs, and took extremely low paying jobs to service. For example, an engineer who lost his job, and is now working at MacDonald's is not considered as part of the unemployed, although the truth is, he more than likely can't maintain his lifestyle on his new much lower salary. The Bureau of Labor Services apparently has another category it puts unemployed people in, which changes the real numbers of unemployment. Keep in mind, **in the Great Depression, unemployment was around 25%**. How far are we really away from calling this a depression versus a recession?

So, for the huge number of people living on unemployment, or not lucky enough to be receiving unemployment, paying credit card debt, as well as other unsecured personal debt, is no longer remaining a choice.

If you want to see something sobering, take a look at **usdebtclock.org**, where it shows, in real-time, the US National debt, as well as the debt per citizen. As of the time of this writing, the ***average debt per citizen is around $52,000***. That's the national average, so never has the time been better for all of us to start being cautious and getting rid of the debts we have.

On a radio interview that I did this month, the host said; "It's because of people like you, that people like us have high interest rates!" I immediately replied; "Who's us? I'm gathering you are not referring to the 30 million or so unemployed, who are not in that position by choice? Debt settlement is a legal option in this country, one which we are allowed to exercise." To which the host stammered, and then changed the subject.

This book was written for the people who no longer have choices. It's not meant to be a blueprint to "cheat" or "steal" from the credit card companies, as certain folk would believe.

This is a strategy, a blue print which offers you a way out of the hole. My choice is negotiating settlements versus declaring bankruptcy for a number of reasons that I will cover in later chapters.

A few weeks ago, while I was attending a religious service, I learned that the person next to me had suffered a heart attack within the last 18 months, as well as suffered a severe decline in income, as he was a housing contractor. Later that day, shopping at an economy superstore, I learned that the checkout lady lost a great job at a mortgage company, which also refused to refinance her mortgage, so she had to find two jobs to make ends meet. As a result, this lady now works 7 days a week. There are so many tragic stories like that out there. These two people I have described above are not even included in the thirty million that are unemployed. How many have you met that have these sad financial issues lately? So many people have been affected by this economy and are victims of circumstances. It's time for us to help ourselves and each other as much as we can, and I hope that this information will be a benefit to you, especially if you are a victim of the economy, like I was.

Many conservatives will tell you to pay back your debt, by starting with the cards with the highest interest rate. Other advice is to stop extra expenses, cash out your 401k, and many other unappealing ideas. You are not going to get that advice from me.

With that, hopefully this book will help you and many others in the same situation, find relief from the overwhelming burden of debt. With the strategies in here, you can settle your credit card debt without the help of "experts". Now is the time to take control of your own finances, and your life and strive for financial freedom. Never has it been a better time for consumers to stand up to the unfair credit practices of the bank. It is my goal to make this information available to as many people as I can, for the lowest price possible, so here goes.

Chapter 1: Getting into Debt

....

How did we get here?

To start off, let's review where we came from, in order to determine where we are going to. Getting into debt is really easy. I believe, that like any other habit, the urge to spend in this society of instant gratification is high.

Your neighbors get a great new car, and all of a sudden, your 3 year old vehicle doesn't look that appealing to you anymore. You want to start up a new venture, easy, let's just get a loan to get started, and worry about the details later.

My first experience with credit was in the mid eighties, when my very conservative father suggested that I get a card to put my gas on, and then pay it at the end of the month, for the sake of convenience. That went along nicely, until one day at the mall, walking past a glossy department store window, I noticed a fantastic Michael Jackson type leather jacket (it was the mid eighties after all). Thinking about that credit card which was being used for gas, I wondered if it would work to pay for that expensive jacket. To my great surprise, the store clerk was very happy to receive payment through that piece of plastic. From that point on, a series of unhealthy credit habits developed.

If you're reading this, it's **unlikely that you owe $500 or so** on credit. **It's more likely that you owe anywhere from $10,000 to several hundreds of thousands of dollars** on credit cards, credit lines, and various other unsecured credit sources. I did. It went way after just wanting small things. It involved changing careers, starting new ventures, refinancing homes, and a multitude of other events which caused lines of credit to be utilized. What I did not realize, and perhaps you the reader can relate to, is how easy it is to accumulate very large quantities of debt. With high mortgages, credit lines with high interest rates, you're pretty much married to your job with the fear of if you lose your income, you lose your home. That, along with the **fear of the unknown** of what happens if you don't pay your credit card bills, **can pretty much keep you frozen in fear, and keep you paying those minimum payments every month**.

The bleak truth is, if you're laden with debt, it's more likely that your cash resources are low and you're in over your head with your mortgage because you refinanced a couple of times, and the chances of having the cash to pay your creditors are diminished. When times are tough and you have to pay the mortgage, utilities or other household items with your credit cards (because of a lack of cash), keeping up with the repayments become almost impossible. At this point, it is seriously time to take action to change your life. There's no happiness in being laden with debt. I had many a sleepless night pondering my dire financial situation, which was also no fun for my spouse, who was trying to get a good night's sleep.

Some of the ways that people get into debt are lined with good intentions. For example, someone starting a new business or venture, needing the initial startup capitalization, will get a line of credit from the banks, in the hopes that the business will take off, to be then able to repay the loan. If things do not go as planned, there is a debt that needs to be paid back, with no apparent income coming in. Another way could be an unplanned health issue, with a few trips to the hospital, and suddenly, one could find their selves in serious trouble financially.

We could blame the lenders that it's their fault for tempting us with those teaser rates, when the truth is it really is our own poor spending habits that got us into trouble.

What options do you have to resolve your debt problem?

Here are a few methods to consider to resolve your debt problems, before you read on to my method. Many people have varying opinions on how to resolve financial issues, but the truth is, when you are in so deep, you really have only a few options.

- **Keep paying.**
  This option is for people who have very high debt and a great income. The downside is that no matter how much money you make, you keep paying and paying the minimum payment. That's what happened to me. I made great money, but could not come out every month due to the huge credit card minimum payment. I was working for my house and my credit cards. Those were my real bosses, which kept me in misery working to make money with no end in sight. Paying the minimum balance every month prolongs your agony indefinitely.

- **Deplete your 401k account and have nothing for your future**.
  This option really makes me sad, as so many people have emailed me to say they were convinced to do this by collection agencies. Make a habit to never touch your 401k. Pretend it isn't there when considering your options. You desperately need your 401k for retirement. There are studies which say almost 50% of baby boomers will deplete their savings within ten years after retirement. Those people will depend on their children to support them.

- **Empty any savings you might have to give to the credit card companies.**
  Personally, I don't like the idea of having no emergency money. How about you?

- **Get a consolidation loan.**
  There are companies out there that will consolidate your loan into one payment, and possibly give you a good interest rate, so you can keep paying and paying. I struggled to find one, but you could have better luck.

- **_Transfer your high interest credit cards to lower interest cards._**
  This is a cute game that many people get lured into by those great introductory rates of 0%. All goes well and life is grand for about 6 months, and then the rate jumps to 11%. Then you can find another card and move your balance to there. You can keep doing this for several years as I did, and continue under the false illusion that you are improving your financial situation. The truth is, that you are just prolonging the inevitable. Eventually you will wear out all the balance transfer offers, and the interest rates will jump, leaving you in the same original situation.

- **_Go for Consumer Credit Counseling._**
  This is a good one. You will sit in front of someone and hand over your credit cards so she or he can cut them up. They will call your bank and tell them you are participating in Credit Counseling which will show up on your credit report for anyone to see, which is a nice reminder to any prospective lender that you can't manage your debt. Then, they make you give them a combined payment, which you send to the Credit Counseling Office, and they then forward to the individual banks. What they don't tell you in the meeting that it takes almost 90 days for the banks to receive your first payment, and your credit is completely dinged anyway. Once again, I tried this, and gave up after about 18 months, and had to pay someone to repair my credit so I could get a mortgage.

- **_Pay off the smallest balance first, and when that is paid, move onto the next balance._**
  This method is to pay off one credit card first, then use that monthly payment on top of the next credit card payment to pay off the second card. When the second card is paid, use that payment plus the first credit card

payment on top of the third payment to get the third card paid off, and so on. Hope this makes sense.

Quick example of 3 credit cards:
- ✓ Discover – Monthly payment $500, with a balance of $2000. You pay this off in 4 months first.
- ✓ Chase – Monthly payment of $300, with a balance of $8000. Add the $500 (from the Discover card which is now paid) to the $300 to make an $800 payment to pay this off in 10 months. Total time so far, one year.
- ✓ Bank of America – Monthly payment of $200 with a balance of $10000, Once Discover and Chase are paid off, you know have $1000 to pay the balance of that off in 10 months. Total time, one year and 8 months to pay your debt off completely.

I paid quite a large amount of money on the internet to buy an eBook to learn about this method and tried it. I calculated it would take about 5 years to pay off my own debt.

- **Bankruptcy.**
  When all your options are completely exhausted, and there is absolutely nothing else you can do, and no other way out, then this is an option. I talk about the downside of this in a later chapter.

- **Debt Settlement.**
  My personal favorite, which is the reason for writing this book. It just makes sense. While there are downsides, the upsides are so great!

The Stress of Debt

Unless someone has actually been through this, and experienced the insane stress that goes along with debt, they can never truly understand what it feels like. I do! I understand what it feels like to not be able to sleep, eat, or enjoy any activities whatsoever because of the huge strain of owing money and not being able to pay. I know what it's like to imagine the worst possible scenario of losing everything you have, or perhaps the embarrassment of your friends finding out how bad your situation really is.

Stress is so bad for you. It can kill you. *It's the most major cause of all health problems.* Here are some of the examples of what stress can do to you;

- It can cause digestive disorders like upset stomachs, ulcers, diarrhea and irritable bowel syndrome
- It can cause you to have accidents while driving or operating machinery.
- It can lower your immune systems, causing you to become more vulnerable to many illnesses
- It can cause your hair to fall out, and many other skin problems
- It can cause chest pains, and heart attacks
- Depression, suicidal thoughts, anxiety, loss of appetite, weight loss, headaches

There are so many more items, that it could take up an entire book, and that is not what the subject of this book is.

At one point, I found myself asking my husband if "death cancels all". Can you imagine, contemplating such an extreme over credit card debt? It's crazy. The turning point for me happened one day when I sat back and said (to no one in particular) "What's the worst that can happen? Come and get me!"

Guess what happened? Nothing! Nothing happened. The FBI didn't show up and arrest me. Neither did the men in black (or white) show up. Once I stopped allowing debt to dominate me, I was able to start formulating a strategy to take back control of my life.

Dealing with the Stress of Debt

You need a definite plan to deal with the stress that you will go through during this process. Getting calls daily from credit card companies and collection agents will wear you down.

Here are some suggestions for you;
- Take care of yourself by getting sleep and watching your diet.

- Organize your life, and don't leave anything to chance.

- Learn some stress management techniques that you can practice every day, whether it's breathing exercises, meditation, yoga, looking at the ocean. Do whatever works for you. Some people get calm by listening to music, or sounds of nature.

- Utilize time management strategies and set goals. Even if you're unemployed and sitting home every day, you can still make yourself chore lists and to-do lists, and establish routines to follow.

- Allocate time everyday to deal with your debt issues. For example, every day from 8:00 am to 10:00 am are the times allocated to communicating with creditors. Don't take calls from them at other times of the day, because every time you have a conversation with a creditor, the anxiety and doubt of what you are doing will return. Collection Agents are paid to scare you however they can, by making you picture the worst possible scenario.

- Use the "what-if" scenario. Every time you start feeling anxiety, ask yourself "What's the worst thing that could happen from this" and run through all the possible outcomes. With each outcome, ask yourself "*And then what*?" For example:

"I could lose my job." *"And then what would happen to me?"*

"I could lose my home" *"And then what would happen?"*

"I'd be out on the street" *"And then what would happen?"*

"I'm not sure after that..."

It is unlikely any of these terrible things would ever happen. Everyone has family members or loved ones that would never let them live on the streets. So as you come out with each possible "horrific" scenario, nix it. Know that most of the things we fear never occur.

Even though I don't know you, I understand from experience what you are going through, and care about people who are stressed due to overwhelming debt. So please take care of yourself during this process.

Chapter 2: Settling With The Bank as low as 20 cents on the dollar

....

What is Debt Settlement?

Debt Settlement is a strategy used to get your creditors to settle for a percentage of the debt. The settlement can be as low as 20 percent of what you owe. The settlement is a final payment that you will make, once you reach a mutual agreement between the creditor and yourself. Your creditors do not want you to know that you have this option available, and will not even mention it in the beginning when you first stop paying your debts. These companies will make it as difficult as they can, to intimidate you into paying.

In my opinion, the major item holding anyone back from doing this is fear. Fear of what will happen that first month, when you stop paying, the second month, the third month, etc. From experience, I can tell you that nothing happens. If they have your correct phone number, the phone might ring, and you will start seeing an extra line of typing on your statement, politely reminding you that you have missed a payment.

So here are some generic questions covering some of those concerns.

What will happen when you stop making payments on your credit card?

For the first month or two you will get some phone calls from your credit card company. You can answer if you want and just let them know that you don't have the money right now to make *any* payment. If you make a small payment this will only postpone the debt settlement process for you. Don't make any payments at all. It is a good idea to write them a letter explaining why you cannot make the payments at this time. Embellish, talk about bankruptcy, and the dire situation you're in. On each subsequent call, let them know the situation is getting worse and worse. You can do this through the mail if you don't want to do this over the phone. It's always a good idea to send every letter as a registered or certified letter with a signature return slip. This way you will know for sure that they received it. Don't forget to keep the receipt from the post office and make a file for each creditor. More about that later.

Even though you are not making payments the credit card company will continue to add late fees, over the limit fees, as well as the regular payment due, to your account and **your balance will still continue to grow.** Do not concern yourself about this, because the goal of this is to still settle at a very low amount. Keep track of the fees and interest added to your account from the first month you miss your minimum payments. At this time you should be saving any money you have. Keep the money somewhere safe. If you're out of work, you have time to find the money somewhere, family member, spouse etc.

The sixth month is often the magic month. After you've gone 6 months without making a payment of any kind, the creditor will probably be ready to settle your debt during that month, or turn it over to a collections agency. Once it goes to the collection agency it will complicate your ability to settle this debt. The benefit is that it could be settled at a much lower rate than the original creditor, as it was sold for cents on the dollar. If your account goes to an outside collection agency, expect the phone calls to increase. Many agencies have an automated computer dial your phone number. Especially Discover. **I was only 30 days late, and Discover called 5 times a day.**

You should keep on file any letters sent to you in regards to your account.

Sneaky Tip #1 * Note: *I opened credit cards using a cell phone that was later changed, but never updated with the credit card companies, and it was almost lonely with the phone never ringing.* So instead of complaining about the phone calls, change your number. Don't forget that you are going to need to keep in touch with the credit card companies and collection agencies if you intend to settle.

Sneaky Tip #2 Sometimes, if the collection agencies can't find you (you've moved, or sent the bills back as "return to sender"), they might give up and that's the end of the collection for that bill. It's too much of a performance and expense for them to find and pursue you. There's no guarantee on this, but it apparently happens and is more common after the original creditor charges off the account.

Many people do not realize that the further you fall behind in your credit card payments, the more eager creditors are to settle with you. Credit card companies would rather have you settle, than declare bankruptcy where they would then get nothing. You'll need to put money aside for the settlement (or beg and borrow from relatives) while not making payments to your creditors.

If your debt remains uncollected for a long time it also increases your chances of a reasonable debt settlement. *At a certain point of time (usually 180 days – 6 months) the creditor will consider the debt amount as loss to get a corporate tax write-off and removes unpaid debt from the books.* This is known as a "charge-off". The company could keep the debt and pursue legal action, OR, it could sell the debt, generally for around 3 to 11 cents. (This amount varies from different sources). This will allow the company to take a loss on the rest. This doesn't mean you will not be persuaded by the creditor to pay back your debts. The credit company can collect the debt themselves, sell or assign it to a collection agency, pursue the case legally for wage garnishment and sometimes even just do nothing. If you are contacted by more than one collection agency on the same debt, it is a good sign for you. This indicates that, the creditor as well as the first collection agency has given up hopes on you.

Creditors don't want you to know about debt settlement. They will try to make it an extremely difficult solution to pursue. Generally, **creditors won't negotiate with people who are current on their bills**, often **refusing to discuss settlements unless you're at least three to six months behind**.

Capital One is a good example of this. By 99 days past due, they still might refuse to discuss settlements. Just keep waiting, and they will change their tune around 120 days. If they don't, then start pushing the idea of bankruptcy. Chase has also been traditionally stingy with their settlements. I had to wait until my Chase account went into collections before getting offered 16 cents on the dollar, which I happily accepted. The banks need to co-operate, because fees to pursue people are very high, so they hold off doing this for as long as they can. And the longer they hold off pursuing you legally, the better chance you have of a decent settlement.

So, if you're going to settle your credit cards, you need to stop paying all of them and let some time go by. Nothing bad will happen to you in the first six months. They can't put you in jail for not paying. If you insist on keeping one last card, make it the one with the lowest balance and limit. Remember, when you are negotiating, they will pull your credit report and say "Hey, you made a payment to Chase?" or "I see you've been making your car payments". They understand that you need to keep a car above all else, so don't worry when they ask you, just keep up the "in dire straits" tale of woe.

Get everything in writing

Sneaky Tip #3 Never agree to send them payments until you *receive* a letter from them stating that this $4,000 (or whatever your amount is) will be regarded as "payment in full" or "settled", and that this payment completely 100% fulfills your obligations to this debt. If you don't receive the letter then they don't receive a payment. They can quite easily fax it to you. When you pay them, send a money order or cashier's check overnight (if necessary, or your deadline has run out). Do not send a check as this will give them your checking account numbers and somewhere down the line, if you're dealing with collection agencies, that might come back to haunt you. See further instructions below, for dealing with the collection agencies. If the original creditor or collection agency refuses to put it in writing then they aren't serious (yet). *Keep in mind that, once you propose a settlement, you are acknowledging the debt!*

If you are dealing with an outside collection agency (the bank sold the debt to a third party) the rules are the same. But before settling with a collection agency contact the original creditor first and make sure that you can't settle with them directly. If they say "NO", because they sold the debt, then deal with the collection agency. There should be no grey area. What if you receive a letter from the collection agency stating that $4,000 is payment in full for a $10,000 debt and you pay them, but the bank (original creditor) comes back later and bills you for the remaining $6,000? So ensure that dealing with the said collection agency satisfies this debt in full. Get the agreement in writing and keep every letter. Once again, don't forget to send all letters registered/certified and keep the receipts.

What happens to your credit score

Settling your debts **will** affect your credit score. Your score is already affected because of the months you went without making payments. It may be further damaged by creditors reporting that your account was "settled". This will lower your score even further. Remember, this means that on future loans you will pay higher interest. That's why getting the "<u>paid in full</u>" or "<u>paid as agreed</u>" is so very important (although not always possible). Once all these items are taken care of, your credit score will start going up again and you can begin on the road of disputing your credit report to remove the negatives. As the debts get set to zero, your score increases. My personal credit score dropped by 45 points which is a lot better than I expected.

The goal of debt settlement

The goal of debt settlement is to have the bank accept a partial percentage of what's owed. For example, if you owe them $18,000, maybe they will accept $4,000 as payment in full. They would rather get $4,000 than nothing at all. Now this won't work if you don't have any money to offer them. So you must have cash somewhere (borrow from parents, spouse, friends – if you have to) that you can use to meet this $4,000 obligation. The purpose of debt settlement is to keep you from having to file bankruptcy. If you file bankruptcy then your creditors will most likely end up receiving nothing and it never looks good on that employment sheet when they ask "Have you EVER filed bankruptcy". You also want the creditor to send you a letter stating that this $4,000 is "payment in full", if they agree to this. They can verbally agree to settle your debt, but if you don't have this in writing you could be in trouble. They might just send you a bill for the remaining $14,000 and act as if they don't recall the conversation.

You want your credit score to remain as high as possible, but don't let this stop you pursuing the best settlement that you can get. Your credit report will more than likely indicate that the account was settled for less than the full amount, if you are unable to negotiate "Paid in full". Remember, if you have the money to settle the debts then you are in control. Let the settlement and negotiations be on your terms.

Getting Started:

1. Create a Folder for each debt. Include in that folder the first statement that you received before you went delinquent (or missed a payment). It might be very useful to get a credit report if you have somehow forgotten whom you owe, and how to get hold of them. You will definitely need to monitor your credit report for later on in the settlement process. Make a list of your creditor's phone numbers with the account numbers and balances, and keep it on a notice board close by to you, where it can easily be accessed.

2. Keep each credit card company in a separate folder. You could also keep all your statements in one folder which says "All Credit", which is the way I did this.

3. Keep a calendar so you can monitor where in the debt collection process you are. When you are on the phone to the creditor or collections department, ask them how many days late you are. They might say 99 days late as of today. Take note of that, so you know exactly where in the process you are, and when to start pushing for a settlement. I updated my iphone with the 180 day mark, and also asked the collection agent on the phone, frequently, as to how many days late I was.

4. Decide on the priority of your debts. What comes first, what comes last. For example, roof over your head (high), utilities (high) food (high) car (high), everything else (not high). Obviously if you are currently in some medical treatment that is necessary, you will have to keep that up too. Keep in mind, when people lose their jobs, the first thing they stop paying, is their credit cards.

5. Keep every written correspondence between yourself and the credit card companies (or collection agencies working on behalf of the credit companies). Try and get everyone's name who you talk to, and add that to the log.

6. Keep a log of every phone call between yourself and the credit card companies (and collection agencies), which will show date, time and context of the conversation
7. Keep copies of the settlement checks, your statements with zero account balance, as well as the envelopes which were sent and received. You might need to correct your credit later on if it does not show a zero balance on your credit report. If you are sending by registered mail with return receipt, then keep that receipt.
8. Study the Fair Debt Collection Practices Act FDCPA. (You can get the link to this from my website www.onlinedebtsettlement.info/resources) This is in case you have to represent yourself if you get sued. (This is a tough one). Monitor your conversations and letters from the lenders, collection agencies for violations of this Act. Google the FDCPA manual to read that as well.

The First Missed Payment

This is 30 days after the first payment is due which marks the date of the First Delinquency. (This marks the start of your calendar of collections) Do nothing at this stage.

Overall Basic Tips for First Few Months

1. **Don't be too eager to mention debt settlement yet:** The idea is to let them know you are in a dire financial situation. You want to be negotiating until you arrive at an agreement that suits you. Show less interest in settlement of debts and try to allow the creditor to pursue the matter. Bring up the topic by simply telling them you just have no money, no job, considering bankruptcy and MAYBE you can find some money from a family member or friend, but you're not sure at this stage. *This is just an example of what you could say. Your hardship story is your own, and it needs to be convincing.* Also let them know, due to your dire circumstances, you won't be able to make a payment. If the creditor knows all you're trying to do is settle, it may not be beneficial to you, and then you may not get a settlement in your favor. Don't use the word "settlement "at this stage. Rather just give them your tale of woe.

2. **Threaten the creditor with plans of bankruptcy:** Approach the creditor in a manner that he is convinced about the fact that you have got very little money, and are on the verge of bankruptcy. Talk to them as if it is their last chance, as you are completely out of options, to come to some type of agreement (settlement). Automatically they will be alarmed. After all, if you file bankruptcy they will get nothing.

Month 2 – 4: Call them up, when they send you letters stating you're late, and to please call them (the creditor). Examples of what you can say: You lost your job (this is a good one which will bring you sympathy up to about the end of month 4). Start offering settlements by saying "If I could come up with a lump sum of money, what you could do for me?" Bank of America immediately offered me 40% (Times are tough, and with 700,000 a month losing their jobs, credit cards are the first thing they are not paying). Try not to use the word settlement, until you are right near the end of the process. It's better for you to pretend you don't know how the game works. You need to impress on them, you have absolutely no money, and there is no money in any type of assets, and you might have to declare bankruptcy. Use the word bankruptcy often. Example, when you're talking to them: "I just don't know what to do. I am in dire financial straits, and I might even have to consider bankruptcy". Do not let them know you have a spouse with lots of money, a rich uncle, and a bank account in another bank that you are using for savings, or any information that they can use against you.

If you have an account at the same bank as your credit card, immediately cancel that account and move your money before stopping paying on the cards. Chances are you are very low on your cash if you are reading this.

Example: I had a Bank of America business, savings and personal account, and then, a number of Bank of America credit cards. First thing was to close all Bank of America accounts. Later on during the process of collections, Bank of America informed me about the "Right of Offset" law.

Here is a brief explanation of the Right of Offset Law:

If you have checking and savings account where you also have a loan, credit card, etc. and stop paying, more often than not, the "right of offset" will apply. A bank can take the money you owe them from your checking, savings, or investment account, to pay any delinquency which has accrued. This ability of the bank to take such action is referred to as the "Right of Offset."

When to start making offers to creditor (after at least 4 months have gone by):

If the creditor is interested in your offer, then make sure you obtain a written agreement including the terms and conditions for payment. The very first time they make an offer, you can say you'll think about it and will call them back. Let some time go by, and call back and say "where were we on the last discussion about a lump sum settlement?" You need to come across as an ignorant consumer (not a clever crafty debt settler), and you want that final offer in writing. Always sound innocent, sad, helpless, depressed, sigh a lot. It works! After about 120 to 150 days, you want to initiate the idea about settling directly with the creditor. By this stage you will have called several times, staying in touch, and politely letting them know you are definitely thinking about them. I opened up the conversation (very politely) by saying "I've heard you do some type of settling. Is that true? Would something like that work for me?"

This is an example of a typical phone conversation you should be having with the creditor by months 4 onwards:

Creditor:	**Hi, is this Debbie Debtor?**
Debbie Debtor: Hi, Yes	
Creditor:	**I'm calling from XYZ Bank to remind you have a payment outstanding of $1200, will you be making a payment today?** *(Same script every time)*
Debbie Debtor:	Unfortunately not. I am still unable to make a payment due to (I'm still unemployed, considering bankruptcy, have no money coming in, all my money is going into my mortgage etc). By the

way, if I could come up with some money by borrowing it from my mother, who is retired, do you have any type of program where I could pay it off with one bulk sum? I believe it's called settling? Would something like that work for me?

If the timing is right, and you are far enough delinquent, creditor will respond:

Creditor: **Yes, we do settlements**

Debbie Debtor: Well, what kind of settlement could I get?

Creditor: **Let's see, on your balance, we could let you settle for 45 cents on the dollar.**

Debbie Debtor: Gee, I can't afford that much right now. Let me think about it

On the next call, you offer 20 cents again, and they might come down to 35 cents. Just keep going. Remember you have 180 days until charge off. Call them every one or two weeks. Start calling weekly around 150 days. If they come up with an offer of settlement that you agree to, then go ahead and accept, and move onto the next debt.

Note: They might even bring up the subject first, around 90 plus days by saying "You know, you can do settlement on this account?" If you hear that early in the process, you can jump for joy, because the home run is in reach!!

Month 5: Now it will be assigned to "Account Managers" for your case or so they say. When you get through to this person, they start off by nice, and then they get nasty. Start offering more settlements. In this month, Bank of America dropped to

30%. This is when to start writing letters of offer settlements. *See samples in Chapter 6.*

Month 6: This is usually the month it gets charged off, and might be your last month to negotiate directly with the bank. You say "If I can come up with the money, say a loan from a family member or friend, what is the lowest you could settle for" The Account Manager says "30 (or 25 or 20) cents on the dollar" You say "Great! Could you send me a letter stating the debt settlement" The Account Manager will say "I am giving you a verbal agreement, and if you send me a minimum payment, I will send out the Debt Settlement Letter".

DO NOT SEND A MINIMUM PAYMENT!!!! THIS IS A NASTY TRICK AND WILL MAKE THE PROCESS START ALL OVER AGAIN

GET EVERYTHING IN WRITING!!!!!

Why the Last Two Days of the month are VERY important:

This is when you will get your best deals, because collection agents get paid commissions on what they collect. So keeping this in mind, press for good settlements on these last 2 days.

Contact Tips

- **General Theory of debt settlement:** The theory is you need to stop paying all credit cards at the same time, else the credit card company will not negotiate if they see you are keeping other cards current. *Note: I started not paying Bank of America 5 months before defaulting on the other cards. Bank of America starting offering 40 cents on the dollar by the 3rd month and 20 cents on the dollar by the 5th month. According to many debt settlement theories, you are supposed to stop paying all credit cards simultaneously as it is a better negotiating* *technique. However, in this instance, it did not seem to make a difference*

How should you contact your Creditors:

- Contact the creditor either by phone or by letter. However, it's better to write a letter (certified or registered mail) as you can attach relevant documents with your offers of settlement.

- **Keep Records of who you are in contact with:** By keeping good records while settling your debts are very important because each conversation you have, you want to know where you left off. You also want to keep any documentation sent to you by the creditor, as well as the envelopes the document arrived in, as this shows the date it was sent. You may need to refer back to the documentation in case the creditor "forgets" the agreement they made with you. It's unlikely the original creditor will try any shenanigans, but keep everything you send and receive anyway. Ask for the mailing address, fax number of your creditor along with the first and last name of the representative and his direct telephone number. You'll need these details if you'll have to contact him again. Try to stay with the same person, because they will keep passing you to different collection agents. They usually take notes, so the next agent can pick up where the last left off. Remember, gentle persistence pays off.

- **How to speak to creditors on the phone:** Be polite while you explain your situation even though the creditor may be rude and offensive. Creditors will not be willing to help you if you're getting irritated and angry with them. They are just people doing their job. It's nothing personal against you. Their only job is to get money out of people, so you want to be agreeable and get them on your side. *Although in these times in 2009, they'd be crazy not to negotiate with 700,000 people a month losing their jobs. Note: I had a very friendly gentleman who specially called back to say he had got 20 cents on the dollar even though it was only 120 days after delinquency. This particular gentleman had a very pleasant conversation with me, and went out of his way to help, because I was very friendly in return.*

What you can tell creditors: Explain your financial situation clearly and inform the creditor about the following:

- Why you're behind on payment
- Your current income & obligations (Here's where you can say you're unemployed.etc)
- Your intent to get current on your debts if you can. (Hopefully, you're going to reduce those babies to 10 to 30 cents on the dollar)
- You're in dire financial straits, and cannot pay the full amount.
- You can't make a payment now, and you don't know when you will be able to
- You may very well be considering bankruptcy and you're insolvent
- You have absolutely no money left, and you can't pay anything.

- o Try not to give any personal information out of any monies you may be earning or have access to.
- o Make the creditors do their own investigations. Remember "Loose Lips sink Ships". So don't volunteer any information, just keep to your script. If they ask you to send bank statements, or 401 plan statements, don't!

Some Cautions:

1. **Don't take out big cash advances right before you stop paying your credit cards.** It can look like fraud and make the lenders want to especially legally pursue you. Even if you're trying to do a bankruptcy, this will count against you. **Sneaky Tip #4** If you plan on stopping paying, and you have made a large cash advance, or transferred a big balance from another card, keep paying that card for several more months until it looks like it wasn't a fraudulent move on your behalf. Morally, ethically, this is not great, but then, hiking your rates to 30+% interest because you were 1 day late on the payment, isn't that great either.

2. Don't give any information to the lenders that will give them any clue as to where you might have money stashed. If you say "I have absolutely no money left" (which is what I did), they might ask "Well how are you surviving", and vaguely answer "I'm barely, or I'm not". The whole object is to make them give up on trying collecting from you, because there is nothing to collect (your bank accounts are empty, you're insolvent, etc). This might help them to believe you're *judgment* proof, and there would be no point in pursuing legal action against you.

3. *There can be tax consequences.* **See Chapter 7 for details.**

4. There is a possibility you can get sued. Anyone who says you can't is not being truthful. Many debt settlement companies and "debt settlement guru's" claim that there is only a 1% chance you might get sued. I wouldn't particularly hug that percentage. It seems that in this economy with six million plus being unemployed (as of mid year 2009) that it would behoove the credit card companies to get any kind of settlement they can. Legal action is expensive. If the main creditor sues you, they have a better chance of winning than if the collection agency sues you. There are many more grey areas with the collection agencies getting them to validate the debt and prove that it's your debt,

produce statements confirming that. **One tip I did pick up, was that if the original creditor turns over the debt to lawyers who act as collection agents, and those lawyers are local to you, there is a good chance of legal action.** If the lawyers doing the debt collection are far away, different states, etc, then all they are doing is acting as collection agents. *It seems very unlikely, if legal action is going to be taken, that it would happen before the 6 month mark (180 days), which is at the charge off point for these credit card companies.* I suggest, if that does happen, to seek legal advice from lawyers who specialize in protecting consumers against credit card companies and collection agencies.

5. If you discover a default judgment against you and you were never notified of the court hearing, immediately contact the clerk of the court for copies of the court documents. Look over the documents carefully for any incorrect information. If you can show the court that you were not given due process, you stand a good chance of having the default judgment overturned. *Please check all the above with an appropriate attorney. This is not legal advice.* (Wikipedia definition: **Default judgment** is a binding judgment in favor of the plaintiff when the defendant has not responded to a summons or has failed to appear before a court of law.)

In conclusion to this topic, if you do get sued, my advice is to get yourself a lawyer. Just remember the old adage "The man who represents himself, has a fool for a client".

In Summary:

This is a long chapter, so to summarize;

1. Be organized and systematic in your approach to this process.
2. Start negotiating after 90 days.
3. Get caller ID on your phone, so you can screen your calls.
4. Read up on the FDCPA so you know what rights you have as a consumer.
5. Always get your settlements in writing, no matter what they say.
6. You don't need to give them personal information such as your bank account numbers and tax returns. Remember, it's an unsecured debt.
7. Don't take out cash advances just before you stop paying, it looks fraudulent.
8. Keep logs of all your correspondence and phone calls.
9. Don't be scared by threats, remember, the collectors will say anything to intimidate you into paying.

Chapter 3: Dealing with the Original Creditor

If the debt is less than 150/180 days, then it is still with the original creditor (the credit card company). Negotiating with the original creditor is different than negotiating with the collection agencies. If you want to avoid having to deal with the charge off on your credit report, then try to settle within the 180 days, so it never goes to a collection agency. To find out if your account is still with the original creditor, call them.

Find out who you are dealing with

When the account is with the original creditor, you still want everything in writing. Sometimes, they will stubbornly refuse, but as time goes by, you'll get your settlements in writing. Just be patient. Remember to monitor for violations of the FDCPA (Fair Debt Collection Practices), and **you can record the conversation if it is not a two-party state.** What this means is that **in some states, you only need to get the permission of one-party to record the conversation, and that one party is you!** As a whole, the original creditor is more ethical than the collection agencies, but to be safe, still follow the rules of paying with a cashier's check. Once you have the settlement from the original creditor in writing, it will stick.

The original creditor will list your account as "settled" and they seem to be quite adamant about that, however, that still looks better than "charged off" in my opinion.

Getting the creditor to make a deal

Keep in mind, each credit company has their own debt settlement policies. The settlement amount differs from one company to another. It is advisable not to argue with a creditor if he is immovable about lowering a settlement amount. Instead you should negotiate with patience and diplomacy while trying to settle on a particular amount. The goal is to work out an acceptable settlement plan with the creditor. *As more time goes by, month by month, that same inflexible creditor will become so much more accommodating.*

The following solutions are what will be offered to you:

One time settlement: It seems to be that you will always get a better deal when you are offering a lump cash amount to the creditor. If you have cash it is possible to get up to an 80% reduction on your debt amount. (50 to 60% seems to be the magic number that they start at) With proper negotiation sometimes it can and will go lower.

3 Month Payment Plan: If you don't have enough cash to offer the creditors a lump settlement, they will give you a choice of a payment plan. Normally, these plans seem to be 3 months, but with heavy persuasion this length of payment time can be negotiated. If you're going to opt for a payment plan, ensure that you have the funds over that time period to pay. If you don't keep to the agreement of the final settlement letter, it can null and void it. So even if you paid $1000 out of the $3000 negotiated, and you break your agreement, the whole balance can become due and payable again.

Bank of America seems to be stuck on a three month repayment plan, if you can't pay all at once. However, if you can, why not just get it over and done with. The settlement made will include your late fees and taxes, although these could also be waived by the creditor.

If you go with a debt settlement company, they can come up with a long term plan, such as three to five years. You end up paying as long as you would if you were still paying the original creditor.

I feel strongly about not using Debt Consolidation Companies. More on that later. Opt for the short plan, and get it over with.

You have the natural advantage in debt settlement, because you have something the creditor wants. ***The longer the time goes by in this process, the better for you.*** Don't give up and get depressed when you don't get anywhere at first. Stay calm and keep your cool. It's usually best to correspond in writing, so you have a paper trail of all your actions. Always remember that your creditor will take less money than the amount they seem fixated on. I had one young lady email me, stating that the bank she was talking to gave her a bottom line to the amount she could settle for. I emailed back that they were lying, and to keep insisting on the lower amount she was offering. The next day, she emailed me to say I was right, and she had the faxed settlement letter in her hand! That made me almost as happy as when I received my own settlement letters.

Let's say you owe $10,000 and stop paying, after about five to six months it will be $12,000 (after the bank has added fees and late charges), and they will negotiate the final payoff of around $2,500 (as an example) on that balance. Once the final payoff is in writing, and you complete it, the balance will return to zero. Don't forget to keep an eye on that to make sure. **You might get one or two bills after the settlement from the bank showing your payment and an amount due. Don't Panic!** Apparently they do that before setting the balance back to zero. Just be aware of this, and follow up by checking your balance. After two cycles, your balance should be set to zero. If not, send a letter to the credit agencies, stating that the balance needs to be set to zero.

I recommend settling with the original creditor because it's easier. Once it goes to collections, it is much harder to locate, and keep track of the back and forth documentation. If you can settle for a low amount, why not save yourself the additional hassle? If you really want to settle for lower than the banks are willing to offer, then collections is what you should be aiming for, in order to get the lowest settlement. *You should easily get as low as 20 cents to the dollar in this economy.* I have heard of it going even lower than that (even down to 15 cents) but was happy at the 20 cent mark. I finally settled two weeks before charge off on the largest account. Hold out until right at the last few days of the cycle to the charge off mark, and then get that final settlement.

However, if the banks are refusing to settle, or budging very little, I would suggest letting it charge off, and see if you can get a better settlement that way.

Why to Not use Debt Settlement Companies

These days, everyone and their dog have jumped onto the Debt Settlement bandwagon. There are a number of very fraudulent companies that are getting people to part with their money, and be in a worse position than they were before.

This is how a debt settlement company works. Let's say you owe $100,000 (using a round number) and you decide to enlist the services of a debt settlement company that promises you a 40% settlement. **They then charge you** 15% of what they've saved you (in this case $60,000), which comes to **a whopping $9000.** They force you to pay the $9000 up front, which may take you a while. After you've paid the $9000 to them, you then start working on accumulating the amount for settling. By this stage, a year has gone by, the account is now charged off, your credit is a mess, and you might give up. No refunds! Yes, this is how they work. So if you do feel this is an overwhelming process for you, then give those agencies very careful thought. That $9000 might have been used for your settling, and now you're even further in the hole. *You can do your own settlement yourself! Really!!*

Why NOT to use Your Credit Cards again

You can survive without credit. Don't use your cards while you are in the settlement process. Don't use your cards for several months before defaulting. This will get your creditors angry, as they will perceive this as fraud. It would be something similar to running up debt just before you declare bankruptcy. If you choose to keep one card up to date, don't use it. It's more than likely after 3 months of not paying, that your creditors are going to close or freeze your account so that you can't use it anyway.

You'll be surprised how easily you can survive without using credit. Really! Every time you have the urge to buy something, and you are in the store, take a good long look at the object of your desire, and ask yourself "Do I really need this?" Your goal is to save every penny for settlement, so when the creditor agrees to your terms and dollar amount, you are ready! If the debt is less than 150/180 days, then it is still with the original creditor (the credit card company). *Negotiating with the original creditor is different than negotiating with the collection agencies.* If you want to avoid having to deal with the charge off on your credit report, then try to settle within the 180 days, so it never goes to a collection agency. To find out if your account is still with the original creditor, call them.

A Few Ideas to Keep in Mind

Just remember, collection agents are just people doing their jobs. They get paid to get on the phone and call people. Debt Collectors are people too. How would you like their job of talking to angry, hostile people every single day? *When collection agents talk to someone who is friendly and nice, they will be way more co-operative. So be nice!*

Don't Fall for the in-house collections trick

Some credit card companies will try to scare you by telling you your account has been assigned to a collection agency after 60 days. When you hear this, stay calm, and google the name of the collection agency. It will more than likely be owned by your credit card company. If it's with a collection agency after only a couple of months, something's fishy. If the account is set to charge off at 180 days, why would a company sell the debt, or hire a collection agency so soon? The answer is, they wouldn't. They are just trying to scare you into paying by telling you that your account is now being handled by a collection agency.

Don't Fall for the "Your Account has been selected for legal Action" trick

After around 60 days or so, the collections department is going to start first trying to get you on a payment plan, lower your interest rate, and many other tempting offers. If you go for any of these offers, it resets the clock for default and negotiating, and your settlement plan will go out the window. They also might start saying things like "Your account has been selected for possible legal action". Note the "possible" word of that sentence. It is against the FDCPA to threaten you with legal action. Once again, it's unlikely you would get sued before 180 days go by. I have heard of certain cases with very large amounts of it happening before, but it is very rare. Remember, if you do get sued, you can always call up the lawyers before it goes to court to negotiate a settlement. You would come to an agreement with them, and they would put you on a payment plan. This happened to me long before I knew about settling.

Always open your mail

You always need to open your mail and not toss it, or throw it in a drawer. I was a big culprit of this. I somehow thought if I didn't open it, it would go away. Unfortunately, it never does.

The reasons are:

1. There might be legal action against you, which you need to take care of immediately.
2. Your credit card company may have sent you a settlement offer which has an expiry date.
3. All correspondence needs to be carefully filed to keep you on track with the settlement process.

Chapter 4: Dealing with the Collection Agencies

....

After the 180 days are up:

After about 180 days, companies write off the debt, and either assign the account (assigning means the ability to transfer ownership of the debt either permanently or temporarily) or sell the debts to collection agencies. Most bad debt companies pay or receive literally pennies on the dollar for the debts on which they are trying to collect. The bank will sell the debt, if the debt has a low score and unreasonable expectation of recovery. This is called factoring.

Different Types of Collection Agencies

There are quite a few different types of collection agencies. The following goes over the basics of some of these agencies, so you can be aware of whom you are dealing with.

- **Fee for Service**

   These types of collection agencies get paid a specific amount for collecting unpaid debts. The amount paid to the collection agency would be determined by the amount owing on the account.

- **First Party (The Original Creditor)**

   Many times, the original creditor may have a specific department within their organization which is named something entirely different. You then get a notice from this department and think "Oh No! It's already been sent to a collection agency", when in reality, it's still with the original creditor. Usually, it's very likely that before 180 days have passed, that it's still with the original creditor. If this happens, call the original creditor and check who owns the name of the collection agency you are dealing with. Google the collection agency. You should be easily able to determine if they are owned by the original creditor.

- **Contingency Collections.**

This type of collection agency charges a percentage of the owed amount that they can collect. They work off commissions. You can imagine that it would be in their best interest to collect as much as they can, but keep in mind, something is better than nothing. So always negotiate the lowest you can.

- **Junk Debt Buyers**

These are companies that buy uncollected debt for pennies on the dollar. These junk debt buyers are usually under the jurisdiction of the Federal Trade Commission.

The amount that companies pay for these debts that have been charged off, depend on the age of the account. (Don't rely on this number because it varies. It's just an overall average)

Keep in mind, even if the debt has been sold, the new owner of the debt still has to adhere to the original delinquency date of the original creditor. *The statute of limitations is not reset by the purchase.*
If your debt is an "out-of- statute" debt, they still might try to collect from you with letters. You need to let them know you understate that the Statute of Limitations has passed, and you will use that as a defense in court if you need to. This could make them give up and move onto an easier target. More about the Statute of Limitations in a later chapter.

Can collection agencies sue you and take your assets?

This seems to be a question on many people's minds. I get a lot of emails on this very topic. So here is the answer:

- The Collection Agencies cannot seize your assets, unless there has been a lawsuit against you, and a successful judgment has been awarded to them.
- A third party Collection Agencies also cannot sue unless they own your debt, or have bought it from the original creditor.
- These agencies work off fear, and often lie about you being sued by them just to scare you.
- You are more likely to get sued if the debt is large, and the delinquency recent and they can determine you have assets and income.
- Watch closely as to where a "legal" letter comes from. If it's local, then there is a good possibility you might be sued. If it comes from a lawyer thousands of miles away, it's more than likely a scare tactic. If you do get a letter from a lawyer, determine carefully if it's an actual summons, and not just made to look like one.

Additional Things to take note of with Charged Off Accounts

- Charged off Accounts from the original creditor can be bought for anything up to 12 cents on the dollar (this seems to vary).
- Charged off Accounts that are older, and have been through more than one collection agency could be 5 cents on the dollar or less. Don't rely absolutely on these numbers, but keep in mind, the older the debt, the better the settlement deal.
- Debts that are past the statute of limitations could be a penny or less.

Contacting Collection Agencies

If a collection agency is merely representing the credit card company, and has not actually purchased the debt, then your chances are good of getting a lower settlement.

Some overall basics for collection agencies

1. Don't look too eager too soon to settle.
2. Make sure that you never contact a collection agency initially by phone unless you want them to have the number you called from. Try to make all your communication happen in writing until you are ready to settle, then I advise picking up the phone to communicate with the collection agency directly.
3. *It seems that in most cases, collection agents want to collect the full amount money owed and have no interest in settling your debts over the phone.* This is where you need to **explain your "hardship" to them and use your negotiation skills.** If you are not able to reach a reasonable agreement, simply decline the offer and

inform them you simply cannot meet the terms they are offering at this time.

4. Don't agree to anything until the collector has validated the debt in accordance with the FDCPA and accordance with the FCRA. The collection agency must send you statement within the first thirty days of their initial contact.

5. Many of these collection agents will try to get your bank information or pay stubs. ***Don't give this information to them, as they might find a way to draw the funds from there.***

Sneaky Tip #5 The best time to negotiate is the last 2 days of the month. Collection agents are paid commissions on the debts they collect. So, near the end of the month, they will do whatever it takes to reach an agreement (settlement) with you.

How to deal with Collection Agents

1. When you **contact the collection agency in writing,** make sure that you refer to the debt by using the account number, as well as other details like the correct name and address.

2. **Once again, ask for contact details**: Collection Agents by law need to inform you their real names and the name of the agency they're associated with. Make sure you keep all documentation between yourself and the Collection Agent.

3. Send a **debt validation letter** (see sample below) in order to verify that you owe the money. They need to validate the debt. Ask for proof that this is your debt. This would include copies of statements from the original creditor, the original contract, the creditor's name and address and a copy of the original agreement. I had a collection agency demand payment for a debt from me, and I sent the debt validation letter, and never heard from them again. *Remember, a collection agency could*

randomly draw people's credit, send them collection letters, and if the person pays "Poof" your money disappears into thin air. That agency may have fraudulently collected without permission from the original creditor. So be careful. See more about this below.

4. You can also ask for proof that the account is still within the Statute of Limitations. Why? If you get pursued legally, you can use the Statute of Limitations defense (if it's an old debt) to defend yourself. See the chapter on Statute of Limitations later in the book.

5. The collection agency has 30 days to validate the debt. If it is valid, then contact the original creditor and try to make your settlement with them directly. If the original creditor tells you to only deal with the collection agency handling the debt, then do so. **This is the stage where, if you have enough money, you can start offering a lump sum payment to the creditors**.

How to get the agencies to stop collection calls:

If the collection agencies are making harassing calls, send them a *Cease and Desist Letter* (sample with sample letters) by certified mail (with request for return receipt) asking them not to contact you. Once they receive your letter, they can call you only to inform what legal action they'll take. Note, the original creditor might not be so willing to stop the collection calls.

Keep a log of when you spoke to the agencies, and who you spoke with.

You will find that every time you communicate with these collection agents, it will be someone different. Always try to follow up with a letter.

The longer the debt remains uncollected, the better your chances will be of getting a good settlement. Eventually, the creditor will consider the bad debt a loss in order to receive a corporate tax write-off. This does not necessarily mean that they won't pursue you for the debt. The course of action chosen by the creditor will vary widely between corporations. If you don't have enough money to make the settlement (as is the case with most people in serious debt) then let your creditors know this, and offer them an alternative payment plan. Scare them with possible bankruptcy options. See sample letters.

Use the threat of bankruptcy OFTEN. Use the same strategy as you used with the original creditor. It will be in your best interest if the creditor believes that you have very little money and you are teetering on the edge of bankruptcy. You should approach each creditor as though this is their last chance to compromise, and get something out of your debt, before you declare bankruptcy and they get nothing. If there is very little compromising going on, on the part of your creditor, you could always **pay a bankruptcy attorney to send letters stating that you have retained their services**.

A Few Ideas to Keep in Mind

- **Don't lose your temper or get mad.** This is a tough one, and I fully sympathize, however, it is really important that you stay really calm on the phone, if you do talk to them. **Once again, be nice. It can only add to a better result than being hostile and belligerent.**
- The collection agency could get a judgment against you (as well as could the original creditor). So, be quick and send a debt validation (sample below) to the collector thereby asking them to validate the debt. After that, it might be a good idea to get a lawyer, or just study up on possible defenses if you defend yourself (only if necessary because you are being sued after the 180 days are up). Many people get default judgments without even knowing it, so keep an eye on your credit report. These default judgments can happen by the collection companies saying they gave you notice of a court date, but somehow you never received the notice (because they never delivered it, even though they say they did.)
- **Request that the collection agency fax or mail a statement saying that this settled amount would 100% satisfy this debt**, and that the loan would be reported as 'paid in full' to credit bureaus. (Don't expect this to happen, in that the Fair Credit Reporting Act, states that an account must be reported as "Settled" if it is a settlement") However, it doesn't hurt to ask, just don't expect it. If the creditor advises you that the letter will state "settled in full" or words to this effect, you might have to reluctantly agree to these terms (they are following the letter of the law).
- *Call the original creditor to insure that they agreed to these terms and that the Collection Agency is indeed authorized to collect on their behalf.* Keep documentation of the phone call with relevant information such as who you spoke to, their supervisor's name if possible, and the date and context of the conversation.

- If the original creditor comes up with a settlement amount that suits you, why not take it? You credit will be on the road to repair faster.
- As time passes, the creditors will likely stop calling and the debt will be filed away for future attention.

Why do Collection Agencies call some people and not others?

Although it seems that collection agencies randomly call some people and not others, it is not. There are different factors involved in why some may get pursued more than others. Here are some of the reasons:

- High Credit Score. When people have worked hard to get a high credit score and keep it there, collection agencies know that they will be more likely to pay up, and therefore be a good candidate for paying or settling.
- Low Credit Score. Someone having a low credit score is less likely to pay. The collection agency might try to get hold of you, and then give up after several months, as it is probably not important to you to get a high score and pay at this stage.

Sneaky (and illegal) Collection Agency Tactics

Sometimes, a collection agency (and this happened to me) will look at people's credit reports to find charged off accounts. They then contact unsuspecting people by sending a collection letter *(without the permission of the original creditor)* to try to get payment on the defaulted account. Two things might happen in this case:

1. Once you have agreed to pay, they then contact the original creditor to get their business, by telling them they (the collection agency) have established contact with their customer (you) and that you are ready to pay.
2. They will get you to make a payment to them, and then your money disappears into thin air. *This is a scam, and is another reason why you must always ask for debt validation.* In my case, when this happened, I asked for the debt validation, and never heard from them again. Obviously, the original creditor was not interested in pursuing me, or did not want to do business with them.

Understanding your rights under the Fair Debt Collection Practices Act is a good way to keep collection agencies in check. This is a federal law which offers protection to people from illegal and unethical collection methods. When you get this book, get a copy of the FDCPA so you can become familiar with it. It's on Google. Read the latest version of it thoroughly. Debt collectors don't expect you to even know there is a law protecting you. It is however important if you ever do get legally pursued to know if your rights according to this law, were violated. At least read it through once. It is interesting.

In General, ways to work with a Collection Agency

Don't Bounce Checks: Make sure your check goes through, and there are funds in your account. Bouncing checks is a big problem. It is against the law, and considered as check fraud and you can be criminally prosecuted. If you don't have the funds, just don't make a payment. Certain States Civil codes allow the recipient of the bad check to collect up to 3 times the original amount. You can also possibly get arrested (if you've made a habit of writing bad checks) and sent to jail. It's just not worth it.

Keep the Agreement: If you have finally got to the settlement you want, and have made plans to send payments by a specific date, then keep to that agreement. By not paying when you said you would, you could nullify the settlement agreed upon, and make them angry. Keep in mind, you can get sued by a collection agency, although not frequently, it is possible. Besides, after all the energy and effort you have put into the process, why would you want to jeopardize that? Rather get it over and done with, so you can move on to the next debt.

How Experian helps Collection Agencies come after you

Experian uses something called "Collection Triggers". What this does is monitor your credit activity. Let's say you were unemployed, and start working again, and making payments. *Experian could send this information on a daily basis to the collection agencies that sign up for their "Debt Collection Tools".*

These collection triggers monitor Charge-off accounts, early delinquencies, and uncollectible post judgment accounts. Any activity on any of these triggers the collection agencies and they come after you. This is something I want you to be aware of. *The Credit Reporting Agencies are not on your side.*

Here is the website URL that discusses the Collection Triggers, and offers the services to Collection Agencies for a fee.

http://www.experian.com/consumer-information/debt-collection.html

My Low Down Dirty Tactic for Dealing with a bogus Collection against me

Once upon a time, I fell for a scam about property insurance on a property that I had owned and sold. *I made the mistake of signing some paperwork,* and then obtained the refund on my own. Years later, one month before the Statute of Limitation expired, they sent this to a collection agency, and it appeared on my report. Being a website developer, I went to Godaddy, and created a free website telling people about the scam of the original company. I also created a website about the company that was collecting on their behalf (the collection agency). When you create a website (about your experience with a particular company) and use a company's name, it jumps to the top of google within days. Within seven days, the collection agency sent me a letter stating they had removed the item from my credit and had dropped collections on behalf of the original creditor. The original creditor sent me a legal letter to stop tarnishing their name, and I responded that if they ever come after me again, the website would again go up within a day. That was the end of that, and I never heard from them again.

Now I'm not advocating you do something like this, but it did work for me. I have used this technique on other occasions to get my money back, when a company did not deliver on their promises. *We can fight back.* Especially as online presence is so important to companies today. By the way, another great resource out there is *ripoffreport.com*, if your web building skills aren't great.

Chapter 5: The Final Payoff

....

Final Payoff Guidelines:

1. Sign your letter. Make sure your name and address are correctly spelled. No nicknames (or put AKA if you have more than one name). Include the correct creditors address, as well as correct collection agency (if the creditor is being represented by one). Also make sure the person signing on behalf of the lender or collection agency is the correct person to be signing and is not the janitor. Most of the settlement letters are from form letters. Include the exact amount that will be settled which will relieve you of any future obligation towards the debt. *See Sample Letters in Chapter 6.*

2. **Don't pay from your normal bank account directly**. (This would include any other online payment that traces back to a bank account. This could come back and haunt you. Pay with a **cashier's check or money order** from a completely different bank than the one you use. I would recommend simply opening an account at a separate bank, then transferring only enough to cover specific checks. These days, this is getting harder to do, but try your best. Just make sure you are not paying from an affiliated source. Draw cash out, and take that cash to a different bank (if you can) to draw up the cashier's check or money order. **Keep in mind, debt collectors can easily track down your bank account from the cashier's check, if it comes from the bank where your checking account is.** When negotiating, creditors can stipulate post dated checks to secure payments on specific dates, don't argue

with this, you could be over negotiating (you already have what you want, don't blow it). A collection agency could request a post-dated check, but they can't demand it.

3. If more than one payment is to be made, make sure the dates of these payments and deadlines are fully understood by all parties. Do not miss the deadline, else they can negate the settlement and keep the monies you have paid, and start the collection process all over again. This is an important point. So take note of it.

4. **Send via overnight mail or other form that guarantees delivery**.

5. If they have a fax, then fax your letter along with all the attachments, if you've come to an agreement. **You also still need to send your settlement letter by certified mail.** This way you have a trace on the mail delivery.

6. If you fax the creditors, keep the fax confirmation sheet. Keep this confirmation as proof in your credit file. Save copies of all your paperwork. These days, even though everything is on your computer, keep all your correspondence to and from the agency in a paper file. It really does make things more organized. This includes a copy of your signed letter with any attachments, fax confirmation sheets, postal certified mail receipts, delivery receipts and return-receipts. The main point is

to stay organized. Keep all your important documents together in your files for at least a year.

Some Cautions:

- Make Sure the Correct Name of the Creditor is on the Settlement letter. Example: Bank of America instead of FIA Card Services
- Try and send the letter overnight to a street address
- Follow up and check that the account is set to zero. This is very important as they could keep sending statements (which they did to me – until I gently reminded them about the settlement). Sometimes it can take the bank eight weeks or so to stop sending you statements and set your account to zero.

Chapter 6: Sample Letters

....

It's recommend you to maintain these guidelines as a checklist while preparing your letters. You need a systematic approach, so there are no future problems while negotiating with the creditors or the credit-reporting agency.

Sample Letters to your Creditors

An unsolicited offer is what you propose to pay your creditors without having an initial talk regarding settlement of your debt. The Unsolicited Offer Letter helps you to have that first written communication on debt settlement with your creditor. You'll find a sample format of the Unsolicited Offer Letter below.

Settlement Offer Letter

Debbie Debtor
123 Debt Street, Debtsville CA 99999
310-555-1212

Acme Collection Agency
123 Acme Street
Creditorville, CA 99999

Today's Date

Dear Creditor,
Re: Account Number_____

Please allow me to explain why I have not been able to take care of this debt. I have been unemployed for 6 months, and have used up all my savings trying to keep up with my bills. Due to this, I have been unable to make payments to you. I am now finally in a position where I can resolve my debt to you for the account number above.

The amount I would propose to pay towards full settlement of this debt is $_____. Currently, I am in negotiations with several other creditors for similar type settlements and have only a limited amount of money available. I have decided to settle only with those that meet mutually agreed upon terms and conditions with me. Additionally, if you would agree to remove any late payment or charge-offs from my credit report, I am willing to offer additional funds.

Please be advised, that I will not make a payment, unless upon written confirmation of this settlement, sent to the address above, or faxed to 310-555-1212. I sincerely would like to settle this debt and have it paid off.

If you find these terms and conditions acceptable, please forward to me, a final agreement. Upon receipt of this agreement, I will forward you the stated amount through a cashier's check or money order.

Sincerely,

Debbie Debtors Signature
Debbie Debtors Printed Name

Another Settlement Offer Letter

Debbie Debtor
123 Debt Street, Debtsville CA 99999
310-555-1212

Acme Collection Agency
123 Acme Street
Creditorville, CA 99999

Today's Date

Dear Creditor,
Re: Account Number 12345678

Due to a long period of financial crisis, I have been unable to make payments to you. To save both of us money and time, I am now finally in a position where I can offer you a settlement towards my debt of which the account number is given above.

The amount I would propose to pay towards full settlement of this debt is $_____. Currently, I am in negotiations with several other creditors for similar type settlements and have only a limited amount of money available. I have decided to settle only with those that meet mutually agreed upon terms and conditions with me. Additionally, if you would agree to remove any late payment or charge-offs from my credit report, I am willing to offer additional funds.

Please be advised, that I will not make a payment, unless upon written confirmation of this settlement, sent to the address above, or faxed to 310-555-1212. I sincerely would like to settle this debt and have it paid off.

Once I receive a settlement letter from you, I will make the first payment within 10 business days. If you find these terms and conditions acceptable, please forward to me, a final agreement. Upon receipt of this agreement, I will forward you the stated amount through a cashier's check or money order.

Sincerely,

Debbie Debtors Signature
Debbie Debtors Printed Name

Countering a Creditor's Offer

A counter offer for debt settlement is what you propose to pay your creditors in response to the offer they made to you. A sample of such a counter offer letter is given below for your reference. It's a good idea to attach this to the Debt Settlement Agreement Letter sent to your creditor.

Debbie Debtor
123 Debt Street, Debtsville CA 99999
310-555-1212

Acme Collection Agency
123 Acme Street
Creditorville, CA 99999

Today's Date

Dear Acme Collection Representative,

Re: Account Number 12345678

I much appreciate that your company is co-operating with regarding a mutually agreed upon debt settlement. However, this amount would not be a feasible amount for me to pay, as I am borrowing the funds from my mother.

Instead, the amount that I could come up with to settle this debt in full would be $_____. Additionally, I would request you remove any late payments or charge-offs from my credit report.

Currently, I am in negotiations with several other creditors for similar type settlements and have only a limited amount of money available. I have decided to settle only with those that meet mutually agreed upon terms and conditions with me. Additionally, if you would agree to remove any late payment or charge-offs from my credit report, I am willing to offer additional funds.

Please be advised, that I will not make a payment, unless upon written confirmation of this settlement, sent to the address above, or faxed to 310-555-1212. I sincerely would like to settle this debt and have it paid off.

Once I receive a settlement letter from you, I will make the first payment within 10 business days. If you find these terms and conditions acceptable, please forward to me, a final agreement. Upon receipt of this agreement, I will forward you the stated amount through a cashier's check or money order.

Sincerely,

Debbie Debtors Signature
Debbie Debtors Printed Name

Sample Cease and Desist Letter

Debbie Debtor
123 Debt Street, Debtsville CA 99999
310-555-1212

Acme Collection Agency
123 Acme Street
Creditorville, CA 99999

Today's Date

Dear Acme Collection Representative,

Re: Account Number 12345678

I would like to request, according to my rights under the Fair Debt Collections Act, that no telephone contact be made by your offices to my home, or to my place of employment.

If your offices attempt telephone communication with me, including but not limited to computer generated calls as well as regular calls and faxes, I will document and forwarded such as a complaint to the Federal Trade Commission.

I would also like to state that I dispute this debt, and request proof from you as to the validity of this debt. Please forward transaction history, as well as statements from the original creditor, including such creditor's name, address and contact information to me.

All future communications with me need to be in writing to the above address.

I would most appreciate your attention to this matter

Sincerely,

Debbie Debtors Signature
Debbie Debtors Printed Name

Sample Debt Validation letter:

Debbie Debtor
123 Debt Street, Debtsville CA 99999
310-555-1212

Acme Collection Agency
123 Acme Street
Creditorville, CA 99999

Today's Date

Dear Acme Collection Representative,

Re: Account Number 12345678

I am writing in response to a notice received from you on January 01, 2010. In accordance to the FDCPA (Fair Debt Collection Practices Act), I request a validation of this debt from your company, which should include the following;

1.   The name, address and phone number of the original creditor as well as statements for at least the last twelve months prior, for this particular account.
2.   I also request a copy of the original signed agreement for my records.
3.   Proof that your company is authorized to collect this debt on behalf of this creditor.

If your office fails to respond to this request within 30 days, this will be construed as a waiver of your claims against me. Please note that this is a request for your company to provide me with evidence and documentation that there is a legal obligation on my behalf. Also be advised that this is not an acknowledgement of this debt.

Sincerely,

Debbie Debtors Signature
Debbie Debtors Printed Name

Follow up debt validation letter after 30 days

Debbie Debtor
123 Debt Street, Debtsville CA 99999
310-555-1212

Acme Collection Agency
123 Acme Street
Creditorville, CA 99999

Today's Date

Dear Acme Collection Representative,

Re: Account Number 12345678

Creditor: Incredulous Credit Card Company
Amount Due: $10,000

Dear Collection Agent,

This letter is to inform you that it has been over 30 days since my initial request to your company for documentation concerning the validity of the account above.

Please see the attached original copy of request of validation for this account. Up to now, I still have not received any of the information requested from your company. As per the FCRA credit reporting agencies, your company now needs to remove all references of above account to myself.

If you do not remove this account from my credit report, with written notification to me, I will file a formal complaint with the FTC as well as with the Office of Consumer Affairs, and will also seek legal counsel to determine what other options I have available.

I look forward to a speedy response from you.

Sincerely,

Debbie Debtors Signature
Debbie Debtors Printed Name

Removing inaccurate information from your credit report

If you wish to remove inaccurate information from your credit report, you'll need to do so in writing to all the credit bureaus in order to have details from your report deleted. Here is an example of such a Request letter below, in order to have inaccurate information removed.

Sample Request to remove inaccurate information

Debbie Debtor
123 Debt Street, Debtsville CA 99999
310-555-1212

Social: 123-45-6789

Credit Bureau
123 Credit Bureau Street, Credit Bureauville, CA 99999

Today's Date

Dear Sir/Madam,

This is a written request to have your company remove inaccurate items and information from my credit report, and to forward to me the corrected credit report once this is done. This incorrect information has severely affected my chances of getting loans and credit, as well as employment.
I am including with this letter, the proof of the items in dispute, for verification. This will confirm inaccurate details on my credit report.

The following items in error are:

1. This is not my account.
2. The account status of this account is incorrect
3. The information is out dated
4. The following inquiries are more than two years old

I demand these items be investigated and removed from my credit report. I also request that these changes be made within 30 days in order to avoid any further violation of the FCRA.

Sincerely,
Debbie Debtors Signature
Debbie Debtors Printed Name

Sample Expired Statute of Limitations Letter

Today's Date

Debbie Debtor
123 Debt Street, Debtsville CA 99999
310-555-1212

Acme Collection Agency
123 Acme Street
Creditorville, CA 99999

Today's Date

RE: Account 12345678

Dear Acme Collection Agent,

This letter is in response to your phone call dated January 01, 2010, concerning the above account.

I also have verified that the Statute of Limitations for enforcing this debt through the courts in California has expired. Should you decide to pursue this matter legally in court, I intend to use the "statute of limitations" defense.

I also hereby request that you cease and desist all contact with me regarding this debt. You may only contact me to advise that collection activities are being terminated by your company.

Be advised that any other communication would be in violation of the Fair Debt Collection Practices Act and will immediately be reported to the Federal Trade Commission.

Debbie Debtors Signature
Debbie Debtors Printed Name

Note: When sending an expired Statute of Limitations letter, it implies the debt is yours and is valid and that you have acknowledged that. Always send your expired Statute of Limitations letters via "return receipt requested", and keep copies for your records.

Chapter 7: Reasons not to file bankruptcy

....

Keep in mind, these are reasons found from my research. Please always check with a lawyer. Find one that will give a free consultation, and try to speak to the actual lawyer and not the paralegal. Also check with the IRS publications, and even call the IRS. They won't ask you any questions about who you are, but will put you through to a specialist in whichever area of taxes you are concerned about, and you will get the MOST accurate advice from them. I strongly recommend you calling the IRS, as you get so many different opinions from so many different people.

The following is my amateurish description of bankruptcy, and further down, is the Federal Trade Commission's description.

What is bankruptcy?

Bankruptcy is a federal court process wherein a debtor gets the chance to eliminate or reorganize his debts through sale of assets or by following a repayment plan. You can file either Chapter 7 or Chapter 13 personal bankruptcy depending upon your financial situation. The Bankruptcy Abuse Prevention and Consumer Protection Act of 2005 (Bankruptcy Reform Act), made many changes in bankruptcy law:

Chapter 7 bankruptcy filing can allow many debts to be eliminated, but personal assets need to be liquidated to pay down some of the debt. This is done by a bankruptcy trustee, who then uses the proceeds to pay creditors. Chapter 7 filers may be allowed to keep any money or property they obtain after filing. Chapter 7 bankruptcy can be filed once every eight years.

Chapter 13 filing requires the filer to set up a repayment plan, typically over a three- to five-year period, but does not erase the debt. The Bankruptcy Reform Act of 2005 states that anyone with income above the state median will have to file for Chapter 13 and pay back at least some of their debts. Chapter 13 bankruptcies can only be filed only if the debtor received a discharge more than two years ago.

7 Great Reasons to avoid filing bankruptcy.

1. **Your credit is hit**: It brings down your credit score. Moreover, the negative entry stays on your credit report for 10 years (Chapter 7) and 7 years (Chapter13) making it difficult for you to qualify for new loans and credit.
2. **Loss of your assets**: There are certain assets which cannot be protected under bankruptcy laws.. This is so because the assets are sold off (if you've filed Chapter 7 bankruptcy) to pay back what you owe.
3. **Not all debts can be eliminated**: Back taxes, student loans and other unpaid dues. Check IRS manuals for more information.
4. **Your finances are horribly affected**: You may have difficulty buying a home or renting (imagine explaining to a Landlord you filed bankruptcy because you couldn't afford your bills). Also difficult to buy a car.
5. **You have to go through a Nasty Means Test.** The Bankruptcy Reform Act of 2005 enforces people filing for Chapter 7 bankruptcy to qualify with a difficult means test (especially if you are married, and one spouse wants for file, but the other doesn't) For Chapter 7 or Chapter 13, you must undergo credit counseling six months prior to filing for bankruptcy and will also be required to take a financial management course.
6. **If you are married, and incurred debts even if your spouse didn't**, in community property states, they will come after your spouse's assets (one of the reasons I did not want to go in that direction). To get around this, you need to file legal separation, and actually prove that you are maintaining separate households. There's no guarantee that the trustee won't seriously question your spouse's assets. Please contact a bankruptcy lawyer about this, because once again, this is a layman overview of the process, and was initially suggested to me by a

bankruptcy specialist. This was an idea that I didn't particularly care for as I did not want to legally separate from my spouse. There are different ways of filing Chapter 7 such as Married, Married filing separate and Married filing separate living in separate household. The first two: Married and Married filing separate do not protect your spouse from scrutiny.

7. **Unbelievable stress:** Your thoughts are consumed with bankruptcy morning noon and night. You are constantly worried about how badly if will affect your future. Once you fully understand how debt settlements work, it is (once again, in my humble opinion) a much better solution, and your credit gets saved.

Debts not considered under Chapter 7: Here are some debts that are not considered under Chapter 7. Once again, *please check with IRS publications*

- Child support
- Taxes
- Liability for injury or death caused from driving in an intoxicated state.
- Student loans
- Criminal fines or penalties
- Non-dischargeable debts incurred from a previous bankruptcy.

Definition: Chapter 7 of the Bankruptcy Code provides for liquidation proceedings to be administered by the bankruptcy cell of the district courts. This means that debtors turns over all non exempt property to a case trustee assigned by the court. The case trustee then sells & converts all the properties to cash & pays back the creditors.

Who's involved in a Chapter 7 Bankruptcy: Apart from the filer, the following parties are involved in the proceedings:

1. Your Creditors
2. A Court trustee
3. Bankruptcy Judge who presides over any hearing & controls and resolves of any disputes related with the case.

Chapter 7 can help in some of the following:

1. Stop Collector harassment: The collectors can't keep on calling or contacting you after being notified by the court after filing.
2. Halts foreclosure: Chapter 7 filing allows one to prolong a foreclosure for a mortgage, until the discharge from bankruptcy is received.
3. Removal of liens: There are provisions for removal of certain liens under Chapter 7 bankruptcy. However, bankruptcy court order is needed for such removal.

In conclusion, there are many different circumstances, which force people to move in a certain direction. I personally don't like bankruptcy because of the stigma, and how long it stays on your record. I don't like the fact that people can easily google you to determine if you have a bankruptcy against you. So, in my humble opinion, use bankruptcy as an absolute last resort. If you have to go in that direction, do so after you know you have tried every other available option to you.

What is the Federal Trade Commission?

The Federal Trade Commission is an agency of the US Federal Government that enforces fair handling of debts and consumer protection laws.

The following information comes directly from the Federal Trade Commission Website, and makes for interesting reading. You need to become as knowledgeable as you can about the laws regarding credit. The more you research, the more confident you will feel.

Here is the website info, and I've included a very detailed breakdown of bankruptcy from them. Also, check on their websites for the latest updates on debt laws, collection agency scams, identity theft and many other useful stories on deceptive debt handling practices.

http://www.ftc.gov/bcp/edu/pubs/consumer/credit/cre03.shtm#FCRA

Bankruptcy

Personal bankruptcy generally is considered the debt management option of last resort because the results are long-lasting and far-reaching. A bankruptcy stays on your credit report for 10 years, and can make it difficult to obtain credit, buy a home, get life insurance, or sometimes get a job. Still, it is a legal procedure that offers a fresh start for people who can't satisfy their debts. People who follow the bankruptcy rules receive a discharge — a court order that says they don't have to repay certain debts.

The consequences of bankruptcy are significant and require careful consideration. Other factors to think about: Effective October 2005, Congress made sweeping changes to the bankruptcy laws. The net effect of these changes is to give consumers more incentive to seek bankruptcy relief under Chapter 13 rather than Chapter 7.

Chapter 13 allows you, if you have a steady income, to keep property, such as a mortgaged house or car that you might otherwise lose. In Chapter 13, the court approves a repayment plan that allows you to use your future income to pay off your debts during a three-to-five-year period, rather than surrender any property. After you have made all the payments under the plan, you receive a discharge of your debts.

Chapter 7, known as straight bankruptcy, involves the sale of all assets that are not exempt. Exempt property may include cars, work-related tools, and basic household furnishings. Some of your property may be sold by a court-appointed official — a trustee — or turned over to your creditors. The new bankruptcy laws have changed the time period during which you can receive a discharge through Chapter 7. You now must wait eight years after receiving a discharge in Chapter 7 before you can file again under that chapter. The Chapter 13 waiting period is much shorter and can be as little as two years between filings.

Both types of bankruptcy may get rid of unsecured debts and stop foreclosures, repossessions, garnishments, utility shut-offs, and debt collection activities. Both also provide exemptions that allow you to keep certain assets, although exemption amounts vary by state. Personal bankruptcy usually does not erase child support, alimony, fines, taxes, and some student loan obligations. Also, unless you have an acceptable plan to catch up on your debt under Chapter 13, bankruptcy usually does not allow you to keep property when your creditor has an unpaid mortgage or security lien on it.

Another major change to the bankruptcy laws involves certain hurdles that you must clear before even filing for bankruptcy, no matter what the chapter. You must get credit counseling from a government-approved organization within six months before you file for any bankruptcy relief. ***You can find a state-by-state list of government-approved organizations at http://www.usdoj.gov/ust/.*** That is the website of the U.S. Trustee Program, the organization within the U.S. Department of Justice that supervises bankruptcy cases and trustees. Also, before you file a Chapter 7 bankruptcy case, you must satisfy a "means test." This test requires you to confirm that your income does not exceed a certain amount. The amount varies by state and is publicized by the U.S. Trustee Program at http://www.usdoj.gov/ust/.

Other Credit Issues of Interest from the FTC website:

Where to Find Legitimate Help

If you're having trouble paying your mortgage or you have gotten a foreclosure notice, contact your lender immediately. You may be able to negotiate a new repayment schedule. Remember that lenders generally don't want to foreclose; it costs them money

Dealing with Debt Collectors

The Fair Debt Collection Practices Act is the federal law that dictates how and when a debt collector may contact you. A debt collector may not call you before 8 a.m., after 9 p.m., or while you're at work if the collector knows that your employer doesn't approve of the calls. Collectors may not harass you, lie, or use unfair practices when they try to collect a debt. And they must honor a written request from you to stop further contact.

Your Access to Free Credit Reports

The Fair Credit Reporting Act (FCRA) requires each of the nationwide consumer reporting companies — Equifax, Experian, and TransUnion — to provide you with a free copy of your credit report, at your request, once every 12 months. The FCRA promotes the accuracy and privacy of information in the files of the nation's consumer reporting companies. The Federal Trade Commission (FTC), the nation's consumer protection agency, enforces the FCRA with respect to consumer reporting companies.

A credit report includes information on where you live, how you pay your bills, and whether you've been sued or arrested, or have filed for bankruptcy. Nationwide consumer reporting companies sell the information in your report to creditors, insurers, employers, and other businesses that use it to evaluate your applications for credit, insurance, employment, or renting a home.

Here are the details about your rights under the FCRA and the Fair and Accurate Credit Transactions (FACT) Act, which established the free annual credit report program.

Q: How do I order my free report?

A: The three nationwide consumer reporting companies have set up a central website, a toll-free telephone number, and a mailing address through which you can order your free annual report.

To order, visit **annualcreditreport.com,** call 1-877-322-8228, or complete the Annual Credit Report Request Form and mail it to: Annual Credit Report Request Service, P.O. Box 105281, Atlanta, GA 30348-5281.

Your Debts and Debt Collectors

You are responsible for your debts. If you fall behind in paying your creditors, or if an error is made on your account, you may be contacted by a "debt collector." A debt collector is any person, other than the creditor, who regularly collects debts owed to others, including lawyers who collect debts on a regular basis. You have the right to be treated fairly by debt collectors.

The Fair Debt Collection Practices Act (FDCPA) applies to personal, family, and household debts. This includes money you owe for the purchase of a car, for medical care, or for charge accounts. The FDCPA prohibits debt collectors from engaging in unfair, deceptive, or abusive practices while collecting these debts. Under the Fair Debt Collection Practices Act:

- Debt collectors may contact you only between 8 a.m. and 9 p.m.

- Debt collectors may not contact you at work if they know your employer disapproves.

- Debt collectors may not harass, oppress, or abuse you.

- Debt collectors may not lie when collecting debts, such as falsely implying that you have committed a crime.

- Debt collectors must identify themselves to you on the phone.

- Debt collectors must stop contacting you if you ask them to do so in writing.

Take Note: See the highlights above. This is why it's so important to keep track of every call made to and from a creditor/collection agency in a log book with the date and time of the call.

Chapter 8: Statute of Limitations

....

Every state has a statute of limitations. This is important because it defines the length of time that a creditor or collection agency can pursue you for a debt.

Example: California Statute of Limitations

Written agreements: 4 years, calculated from the date of breach.

Oral agreements: 2 years.

Look up your state on the web (Just type in Statute of Limitations on Google and it will pop up.

Here's the Wikipedia definition of Statute of Limitations

A **statute of limitations** is a statue that sets forth the maximum period of time that legal proceedings may be initiated.

My layman definition of Statute of Limitations

Statute of Limitations applies to open ended contracts such as credit cards and store credit accounts and contracts for sale under the Uniform Commercial Code. Also covered under most States are oral agreements, promissory notes, written contracts, loans, mortgages and car payments as well as foreign and domestic judgments. Under the right circumstances the statue of limitations can be renewed for just about any type of debt. Statute of Limitations on debt is the legal time limit of the debt. It does not apply to all debts! Learn about your state's Statute of Limitations on debts and whether or not the rule applies to your situation. The debt collector may just be liable to you for statutory damages of up to $1,000, plus any actual damages suffered, plus attorney fees if they pursue you after the Stature of Limitations has expired.

Not all debt has a statute of limitations! Also, *when the Statute of Limitations expires*, it *can be used as a defense* to stop collectors from collecting through the courts. Keep in mind that the debt DOES NOT go away! Collectors can still attempt to collect the debt using other methods

Apparently, there is NO statute of limitations on:

- Federal Student Loans;
- Most Types of Fines;
- Past Due Child Support (state dependent)
- Taxes (Check with a local tax resolution expert about your particular situation.)

Generally, the statute of limitations for collecting debts begins when you sign a credit contract. **Every state has its own specific rules on the running of the statutory period**.

The term "toll" or "tolled" means to **"stop the running of a statutory period for a certain period of time"**. Many states use this term in their statutes of limitation rules and civil codes for debt collection.

The statute of limitation is stopped if the debtor makes a payment on the account after the expiration of the applicable limitations period.

BIG WARNING! While the statute of limitations is running, *making ANY payment can reset or restart the statute of limitations.* Always ensure the debt is valid, and then check your state laws to see if the debt has a statute of limitations BEFORE taking any other action such as making a payment or signing an agreement to make payments.

EXAMPLE: If you got a personal loan on February 1st 2001, and in your state, the Statute of Limitations is three years. Your first payment was due March 1st 2001, but you never paid it. The Statute of Limitations expires March 1, 2004. If you make any payment, let's say two years later for a small amount like $50, it would reset the date and the Statute of Limitations would run for another three years from the date of that payment. This could even allow a collector to seek a judgment against you. Even thought the Statute of Limitations expired, collectors could still try to collect these expired debts and pursue legal action against you. If you use the Statute of Limitations as a defense and you qualify, the case would generally be dismissed. Once again, remember this is my layman interpretation. Please always contact a lawyer who specializes in this topic.

When the statute of limitations has expired, and a collector is after you for a debt, consider sending collectors an Expired Statute of Limitation Letter (see sample in chapter 6) to inform them of your financial situation and that you are aware of the expired Statute of Limitations and will use it as your defense if taken to court. As stated earlier, even though the statute of limitations has expired and you are unable to pay the debt, you can still be legally pursued in court. If that happens, you need to appear in court to use the statute of limitations defense. **You definitely need to talk to an attorney about this. I just want to make you aware that there is a Statute of Limitations in your State.**

Chapter 9: Filing Taxes and Credit Card Debt Forgiveness

....

Hopefully the information below is extremely helpful to you as it is one of everyone's major concerns. The chances are that if you are seeking credit card debt settlement, you probably are insolvent.

Lenders and Debt Forgiveness

1. A lender can report any debt forgiven over $600 to the IRS with a 1099-C form. In the event of this, **you will have to pay taxes on the forgiven amount**. It's still a lot cheaper than paying the whole debt. Keep in mind, this becomes a non-recourse debt, when a company forgives a debt, this becomes a taxable event to you. A debt is "recourse" debt when the debtor is personally liable for the debt. In the case of a mortgage, if the debt is "nonrecourse", the debt is only secured by a property, and the debtor is not personally liable for the balance. For example: Mortgages from refinancing a previous mortgage are usually recourse. For joint filing, this amount will roll into the income of you & your spouse (if you're married), and will increase your income by the amount of the forgiven debt. Just something to keep in mind, if one of you is financially sound, and the other isn't.

2. Let's talk about **filing taxes** with the **credit card debt forgiven amount** from the credit card companies when they send you the dreaded 1099-C in the mail.

3. You first need to **determine if you are insolvent**. You can determine this by adding up your liabilities (credit card debt, loans, mortgages, etc) and subtracting your assets (home, 401k, cash etc). *If your liabilities exceed your*

assets, you are insolvent. You can exclude from gross income, the debt that was cancelled up to the amount that your liabilities exceed assets by using Form 982 (check on the IRS website).

a. EXAMPLE: Let's say you're insolvent by $75,000, and $100,000 of debt is cancelled, you are responsible for the remaining $25,000._ Now it gets complicated if you're filing joint taxes and your spouse has assets, but you don't and you are trying to determine insolvency. Publication 4681, page 6 is the insolvency worksheet to determine your insolvency. If there are jointly owned items just before Cancellation Of Debt, you would have to determine how the state laws apply, and it can differ if it's a community property state (if you are married and jointly own assets). Form 982 is for determining insolvency individually so that any portion of the debt cancelled does not go into ordinary income. I got this information directly from the IRS, but once again, advise you to contact a CPA or the IRS themselves (they really are very helpful).

EXAMPLES FROM THE IRS WEBSITE

Example 1 (Taken from IRS Publication 4681). In 2008, Greg was released from his obligation to pay his personal credit card debt in the amount of $5,000. Greg received a 2008 Form 1099-C from his credit card lender showing canceled debt of $5,000 in box 2. Greg uses the insolvency worksheet to deter-mine that his total liabilities immediately before the cancellation were $15,000 and the FMV of his total assets immediately before the cancellation was $7,000. This means that immediately before the cancellation, Greg was insolvent to the extent of $8,000 ($15,000 total liabilities minus $7,000 FMV of his total assets). Because the amount by which Greg was insolvent immediately before the cancellation exceeds the amount of his debt canceled, Greg can exclude the entire $5,000 canceled debt from income. When completing his tax return, Greg checks the box on line 1b of Form 982 and enters $5,000 on line 2. Greg completes Part II to reduce his tax attributes as explained under *Reduction of Tax Attributes,* later. Greg does not include any of the $5,000 canceled debt on line 21 of his Form 1040. None of the canceled debt is included in his income.

Example 2. (Taken from IRS Publication 4681) Assume the same facts as in Example 1 except that Greg's total liabilities immediately before the cancellation were $10,000 and the FMV of his total assets immediately before the cancellation was $7,000. In this case, Greg is insolvent to the extent of $3,000 ($10,000 total liabilities minus $7,000 FMV of his total assets) immediately before the cancellation. Because the amount of the canceled debt exceeds the amount by which Greg was insolvent immediately before the cancellation, Greg can exclude only $3,000 of the $5,000 canceled debt from income under the insolvency exclusion. Greg checks the box on line 1b of Form 982 and includes $3,000 on line 2. Also, Greg completes Part II to reduce his tax attributes as explained under *Reduction of Tax Attributes* later. Additionally, Greg must include $2,000 of canceled debt on line 21 of his Form 1040 (un-less another exception or exclusion applies).

Please check at http://onlinedebtsettlement.info/Resources.html for links that will take you to the right place in the IRS manual for the above topic.

See the IRS Insolvency Worksheet on the next page from Publication 4681 Cancelled Debt, Foreclosures, Repossessions and abandonment on page 6. Fill in the form and give it to your accountant. Your accountant will take the bottom line, Line 40 Amount of Insolvency, and add it to your tax return.

Chapter 10: I practice what I preach – See my own settlement letters from BOA

··

On the next page is proof that what I've described in this document works. I settled the accounts below for 20 cents on the dollar and it was completed by the 5th and 6th month. Conquer fear, and once you get started, it will get easier.

I used exactly the methods described in this book, with no outside help. If this worked for me, I know it can work for you. Just be methodical in your approach and create a plan and stick to it. If you are worried about what to say to your creditors, one of my readers suggested planning your conversation out in advance by writing it down. Do whatever gives you the confidence to move forward with this. One thing I promise, you won't be sorry did.

The four letters below show a total amount owing of $72,796.94 which was settled in full for $14,800.00 before the end of the six month mark.

www.bankofamerica.com

REDONDO BEACH CA 90277

June 08, 2009

Account No.:

Dear

This letter confirms our conversation to settle the above-referenced account. Your current balance is $19,584.11. We will accept $4,000.00 as settlement on this account. Thank you for your first payment towards this settlement, each future installment is listed below.

Settlement Installment	Installment Due Date
$1,333.00	June 26, 2009
$1,333.00	July 27, 2009
$1,334.00	August 26, 2009

By completing this payment plan, your account will be considered settled. Although this account is now closed, please note that any new or third-party charges posted to this account will be your responsibility. You will not be obligated to pay the remaining balance, provided no additional charges appear on this account after the date of this letter. Also, any future account activity that results in a credit balance will become the property of Bank of America. Any violation of this agreement will result in the full balance being due immediately. All payments must be received by the above stated due dates.

If the remaining amount is equal to or greater than $600.00, we are required by federal law Internal Revenue Service (IRS) section 6050P to report this amount. You will be receiving a Form 1099-C from Bank of America no later than next January 31. If you have any questions regarding your personal taxes, we recommend that you consult a certified public accountant or other tax professional.

www.bankofamerica.com

REDONDO BEACH CA 90277

June 08, 2009

Account No.:

Dear

This letter confirms our conversation to settle the above-referenced account. Your current balance is $14,677.02. We will accept $3,000.00 as settlement on this account. Thank you for your first payment towards this settlement, each future installment is listed below.

Settlement Installment	Installment Due Date
$1,000.00	June 25, 2009
$1,000.00	July 25, 2009
$1,000.00	August 25, 2009

By completing this payment plan, your account will be considered settled. Although this account is now closed, please note that any new or third-party charges posted to this account will be your responsibility. You will not be obligated to pay the remaining balance, provided no additional charges appear on this account after the date of this letter. Also, any future account activity that results in a credit balance will become the property of Bank of America. Any violation of this agreement will result in the full balance being due immediately. All payments must be received by the above stated due dates.

If the remaining amount is equal to or greater than $600.00, we are required by federal law Internal Revenue Service (IRS) section 6050P to report this amount. You will be receiving a Form 1099-C from Bank of America no later than next January 31. If you have any questions regarding your personal taxes, we recommend that you consult a certified public accountant or other tax professional.

www.bankofamerica.com

▬▬▬▬▬▬▬▬▬▬(Business)

▬▬▬▬▬▬▬(Guarantor)

▬▬▬▬▬

▬

REDONDO BEACH CA 90277

Account No ▬▬▬▬▬

Account Balance: $26530.50

Dear ▬▬▬▬▬▬▬▬

Per our conversation, this letter sets forth a proposal to settle the above-referenced account. We will accept 5,400.00 as a settlement on this account. To accept this offer, you must agree to send the first installment payment of 2700.00 by 7/16/09. Each future installment is listed below.

Settlement Installment	Installment Due Date
1. 2700.00	7/16/09
2. 2700.00	8/16/09

By completing this payment plan, your account will be considered settled, and you will not be obligated to pay the remaining balance, provided no additional charges appear on this account after the date of this letter, Also, any future account activity that results in a credit balance will become the property of Bank of America. Any violation of this agreement will result in the full balance of $26530.50 Payment due immediately, all payments must be received by the above stated due dates.

If the remaining amount is equal to or greater than $600.00, we are required by federal law (IRS Section 6050P) to report this amount. You will be receiving a Form 1099-C from Bank of America no later than next January 31 of the next year. If you have any questions regarding your personal taxes,
We recommend that you consult a certified public accountant or other tax professional.

Bank of America

www.bankofamerica.com

(Business)

(Guarantor)

REDONDO BEACH CA 90277

Account No

Account Balance: $11805.31

Dear

Per our conversation, this letter sets forth a proposal to settle the above-referenced account. We will accept $2,400.00 as a settlement on this account. To accept this offer, you must agree to send the first installment payment of $1200.00 by 7/16/09. Each future installment is listed below.

Settlement Installment	Installment Due Date
1. 1200.00	7/16/09
2. 1200.00	8/16/09

By completing this payment plan, your account will be considered settled, and you will not be obligated to pay the remaining balance, provided no additional charges appear on this account after the date of this letter. Also, any future account activity that results in a credit balance will become the property of Bank of America. Any violation of this agreement will result in the full balance of $11805.31 Payment due immediately, all payments must be received by the above stated due dates.

If the remaining amount is equal to or greater than $600.00, we are required by federal law (IRS Section 6050P) to report this amount. You will be receiving a Form 1099-C from Bank of America no later than next January 31 of the next year. If you have any questions regarding your personal taxes,

We recommend that you consult a certified public accountant or other tax professional.

Chase Charges off

The fifth settlement letter here was obtained after my Chase account charged off and was handed over to a collection agency. I was offered 20 cents on the dollar on the first call, and by the second call, I countered with 16 cents on the dollar.

Remember, *when an account is charged off*, this means that the company will show this debt as a bad debt to the investors in that company, and that debt is then used as a tax deductible business expense for the credit card company. Even if a credit card company charges off an account, the debt still remains valid, it can still legally be collected.

The collection agency was surprisingly easy to work with. I did my research, contacted Chase to verify this was indeed the collection agency representing them, which they did. They faxed me the settlement letter, and I checked the wording, and went ahead and sent them a cashier's check by certified mail with a return receipt, so I knew exactly when it was delivered.

VALENTINE & KEBARTAS, INC.

15 Union Street, Lawrence , Massachusetts 01840 PHONE: 1-866-598-2788 FAX: 941-748-0258 EMAIL: lseig@vki-fl.com

February 10, 2010

Redondo Beach, CA 90277.

RE: Chase Bank USA , N.A.
Account Number:
Current Balance: $ 11,544.89
Paid to VKI: $ 2,250.00

Dear Ms.

Valentine and Kebartas, Inc. is a legally authorized representative of CHASE BANK USA, N.A.

We have received a settlement of this liability for the sum of *Two Thousand Two Hundred Fifty Dollars ($2,250.00).*

This payment will represent a settlement in full on the above captioned account; your credit bureau report will be updated accordingly by our client.

Please call 1-866-598-2788 should any further assistance be required from our office.

Very truly yours,

Pauline Reardon
Collections Manager

The 1099 that Bank of America sent after the debt was settled.

The following page shows what a 1099c looks like. This is the document that gets sent to you at the end of the tax year, during which the settlement occurred.

Also, take a look at the 1099c that Bank of America sent me on the January of the year following their forgiven debt.

Keep in mind, this is something you have to deal with, and include with your tax return. You can't ignore it. This is when you fill in the Form 982 that I discuss later, to prove insolvency and forward to your accountant.

BANK OF AMERICA, N.A.
CONSUMER LENDING
PO BOX 22021
GREENSBORO, NC 27420-2021

COMBINED TAX STATEMENT FOR YEAR 2009

THIS STATEMENT REPORTS 1099-DIV (OMB No. 1545-0110), 1099-INT (OMB No. 1545-0112), 1099-OID (OMB No. 1545-0117), 1098 (OMB No. 1545-0901), 1099-MISC (OMB No. 1545-0115), 1099-B (OMB No. 1545-0715), 1099-Q (OMB No. 1545-1760), 1099-A (OMB No. 1545-0877), 1099-C (OMB No. 1545-1424), 1099-S (OMB No. 1545-0997, 1098-E (OMB No. 1545-1576), 1099-SA (OMB No. 1545-1517).
DEPARTMENT OF THE TREASURY-INTERNAL REVENUE SERVICE.

BANK# 7503

*******AUTO**SCH 3-DIGIT 902

PAYERS E.I.N.

CUST SERV PH #
(888) 800-5419

TAXPAYERS IDENTIFICATION NUMBER

"For Form 1099-B, DIV, INT, MISC, OID and Q: This is important tax information and is being furnished to the Internal Revenue Service. If you are required to file a return, a negligence penalty or other sanction may be imposed on you if this income is taxable and the IRS determines that it has not been reported."

ACCOUNT NUMBER	ACCOUNT TYPE	IRS DESCRIPTION	IRS BOX #	AMOUNT
* * * 2009 FORM 1099-C, CANCELLATION OF DEBT * * *				
	CREDIT CARD	AMT DEBT CANCELED	2	15584.11
	06/29/2009	DATE CANCELED	1	
SETTLEMENT DEFICIENCY BALANCE		DEBT DESCRIP	4	
		BORROWER WAS PERSONALLY LIABLE	5	
		FOR REPAYMENT OF DEBT		
	CREDIT CARD	AMT DEBT CANCELED	2	11677.02
	07/03/2009	DATE CANCELED	1	
SETTLEMENT DEFICIENCY BALANCE		DEBT DESCRIP	4	
		BORROWER WAS PERSONALLY LIABLE	5	
		FOR REPAYMENT OF DEBT		

Chapter 11: Disputing Inquiries with the Credit Agencies

....

Every time you apply for credit or when someone checks your credit, a credit inquiry is placed on your file. These Inquiries are shown on your credit report so that potential creditors and lenders can see how often you apply for new credit. The reason why these are not good for your credit report is that it can indicate to the creditor you are trying to get credit from anywhere and everywhere, and that you might be having financial problems. This will have a negative effect on your credit score. The credit agencies have to, by law, keep a record of these inquiries for 24 months. After that, the inquiries should come off your credit reports. Credit Inquiries can stay on your credit report for 24 months, but will only cause your credit scores to change within the first 12 months. Most creditors will ignore inquiries older than six months.

Examples of Hard inquiries

These will cause problems for you and will lower your credit scores, and will be the following:

1. Companies reviewing you for credit or pulling a credit report on you on which you have given them permission.
2. Collection agencies that are trying to collect a debt from you.
3. You apply for credit for a purchase such as a car, or apply for a line of credit or credit card

Examples of Soft inquiries

These won't cause problems for you, and will be the following:

1. Job Application
2. Inquiries from Utility Companies
3. Credit Company that is monitoring and reviewing your account
4. Different Types of Promotional inquiries.
5. Companies pre-screen you for offers, or you request your own credit report.

An unauthorized inquiry is when someone accesses your credit report without getting your permission. In this case, a dispute can be reported to the company that accessed your report. According to the FCRA (Fair Credit Reporting Act) only authorized inquiries are allowed to show up on your credit report (according to Section 604 of the FCRA). If that company does not respond within 30 days, this now becomes a lack of response to a creditor dispute. The credit union will now take the side of the consumer and remove the negative item (inquiry).

At this stage, request if the creditor cannot verify the authorization, they should agree to remove the inquiry and send a letter to you which will state that the inquiry was made in error. If the credit company does not comply, theoretically, you could now use the services of a lawyer to force the issue. You would need to know what your FICO scores are before and after the inquiry so you could sue for damages.

What should you do to remove these inquiries?

Easy, just follow the points below.

1. Order your credit reports from all three agencies and review the hard and soft inquiries
2. Look up the address and contact information of the creditor for each inquiry on your credit report (mostly the ones that occurred within the last year as these are the ones that will affect your credit score).
3. Write a letter to each of the creditors that did these inquiries, asking them to remove the inquiry. Send the letters with certified mail with a return receipt. See the sample below.
4. Write a dispute letter to the credit bureaus and wait for the investigation of your claims. This might take several months, so be patient.
The credit bureaus have 30 days to investigate your claim and respond to you in writing. Once they have completed their investigation, they will let you know of the results and will send these to you in the mail with a copy of your credit report.

You can also dispute online. See Equifax site as an example:
http://www.equifax.com/answers/correct-credit-report-errors/en_cp

Sample Letter to Creditor to Remove Inquiries

Debbie Debtor
123 Debt Street, Debtsville CA 99999
310-555-1212
Social: 123-45-6789

Acme Credit Bureau
123 Credit Bureau Street, Credit Bureauville, CA 99999
Today's Date

RE: Unauthorized credit inquiry

Dear Creditor,

While recently checking my credit report from (name the Credit Agency), I noticed the following inquiry made by your company and would like to bring these errors to your attention.

The following inquiry was made:
(Give details of the inquiry here and be as thorough as you can)

I did not approve your company to make such an inquiry, this inquiry is damaging to my credit score and will have a negative impact on any future credit applications I may make.
As I understand it, you are not legally allowed to make such an inquiry without my permission according to Section 604 of the Fair Credit Reporting Act. I request that you contact the credit bureaus and agencies and have the unauthorized inquiry removed. This inquiry violates the Fair Credit Reporting Act, Section 1681b(c): Transactions Not Initiated by Consumer. Please remove my personal information from your files after removing the unauthorized inquiry from my credit and forward to me a written confirmation that this has been done.

If you have documentation that supports the authorization of this inquiry, then please forward me a copy so that I may verify the validity of this.

Thanking you in advance,

Debbie Debtor's Signature
Debbie Debtors Printed Name

Another Sample Letter to the Credit Bureaus to Remove Inquiries

Debbie Debtor
123 Debt Street, Debtsville CA 99999
310-555-1212
Social: 123-45-6789

Acme Credit Bureau
123 Credit Bureau Street, Credit Bureauville, CA 99999
Today's Date

Dear Credit Bureau,

This letter is a formal complaint that you are reporting inaccurate credit information on my credit report. I very recently obtained my report from your agency and have noted that the following unauthorized inquiries have been made to my credit profile and this has had an extremely damaging affect on my credit standing.

- Example Inquiry 1
- Example Inquiry 2

Because of this, I have been denied credit recently. I am attaching the following letter from the creditor as proof that this was an unauthorized inquiry and would like this to be removed as soon as possible from my credit profile.

The following companies inquiries needs to be verified and deleted from my report:

Acme Credit Card Company
Account Number: 123456758

Please ensure that the following information is removed from my credit profile as soon as is possible

Thanking you in advance,

Debbie Debtor's Signature
Debbie Debtors Printed Name

Disputing Other Items with the Credit Bureau's

It is a good idea to review your credit report often to protect yourself against identity theft, and to ensure that the information on the report is accurate. Keep in mind; most credit reports contain inaccurate information. There are times when you dispute and item, even though you are correct, the original creditor confirms it as valid. In that case, you need to keep disputing with additional evidence. If all of that fails, you can report them to the FTC or OCC, which I talk about in a later chapter.

Reviewing Your Credit Report Frequently

Your credit report contains a lot of very important information about where you live, the timeliness of how you have paid your bills in the past, any bankruptcies and other relevant information to your financial soundness. Any negative information can stay on your report for seven years, and a bankruptcy can stay on for ten years. (Yet another reason not to file bankruptcy).

Debt settlement does have an impact on your credit report. If you should settle before the six month mark when charge offs occur, it will definitely have a better impact on your credit report.

Keep in mind that **eliminating your debt will improve your credit in the long run**. Your credit report may show "settled in full" which is better than showing charged off.

What is most damaging to your Credit Report

- Bankruptcy
- Foreclosure
- Repossession
- Loan Default
- Court Judgments
- Collections
- Past due payments
- Late Payments
- Credit Rejections
- Credit Inquiries

How Long Negative Items Stay on Your Credit Report

Bankruptcy Chapter 7	10 years
Bankruptcy Chapter 13	7 years
Judgment against you	7 years
Foreclosure	7 years
Collections/Delinquencies	7 years
Credit Inquiries	2 years
Charge Off	7 years
Tax liens	7 years

Debt settlement does have an impact on your credit report. If you should settle before the six month mark when charge offs occur, it will definitely have a better impact on your credit report. The older the items are, the less impact they have on your score.

The Fair Credit Reporting Act (FCRA) is there to ensure the accuracy of your credit report, and allows you to dispute items which you believe should not be there. This Act directly affects the Consumer Reporting Agencies as it ensures that the information they are reporting about you is correct. The FCRA requires that each of the credit agencies (Equifax, Experian and TransUnion) should provide you with a free copy of your credit report once a year. These agencies have setup a website for you to obtain these free reports at www.annualcreditreport.com

If you are denied credit, you are entitled to a free credit report by Federal law. You can also get a free report if you're unemployed or on welfare.

You can Repair Your Own Credit Report

Credit repairs charge very high fees to do exactly what you could do yourself. So why not give it a try. There are plenty of great books on the topic, and although I don't go into depth about it in this book, it wouldn't take long for you to find some other detailed credit repair guides out there.

What to do if there are inaccurate items on your report

1. While reviewing your credit report, *if you find errors*, this is when you will **write dispute letters to each credit bureau and to the reporting company**. Keep in mind, that this is all that is done by the companies that charge all that money to fix your credit. Remember to include any supporting documentation as to why you are disputing this item.

2. Send the letter by registered mail (or certified) so that you can keep track of when it was sent. It's preferable not to dispute online, but to do everything in writing, as **everything needs to be documented**.

   See Chapter 6 for an example of a Dispute Letter to the credit bureau's as well as the example from the FTC (Federal Trade Commission) below.

3. ***These agencies need to respond and resolve the issue within 30 days or remove the items.*** They have to contact the original creditor that reported these inaccuracies with what you have disputed. Once the investigation is complete, the credit agencies need to provide you with a free report and the written results if the dispute is accepted, and a change is made to your credit report. You can also send a letter to the actual creditor telling them in writing that you are disputing an item. There's a good chance that your records may be lost or too difficult to find within the thirty days.

4. You can also request that a statement of your dispute be included in your credit report, if your dispute is not resolved by the credit agencies.

5. It's easier to dispute older items (older than 2 years), as the original creditors may not have the necessary paperwork to verify the dispute.

6. In your dispute letter, you could use reasons such as:

   - Wrong amount reported
   - Not my debt
   - Incorrect original creditor
   - Incorrect dates
   - Incorrect status and balance reported
   - Charge off date incorrect
   - Wrong month on late pay
   - Incorrect Account Number

Keep in mind, if you are going to dispute something again, that you need to use a different reason the next time around. This is important because the credit bureau may not take any action for frivolous disputes.

Where should you send dispute letters to?

These are the addresses to write to with your dispute letter:

Experian (experian.com)
P.O. Box 9701
Allen, TX 75013
800-493-1058

Trans Union (transunion.com)
P.O. Box 2000
Chester, PA 19022
800-916-8800

Equifax (equifax.com)
P.O. Box 740201
Atlanta, GA 30374
800-685-1111

If the credit bureau refuses to remove the disputed item, you can file a complaint with the Federal Trade Commission. Although they don't resolve individual disputes, every complaint filed against a credit agency gets that agency investigated and enforces a higher compliance with the dispute process.

Federal Trade Commission
600 Pennsylvania Avenue, NW
Washington, DC 20580
(202) 326-2222

http://www.naca.net/ (National Association of Consumer Advocates) is a website resource that consists of attorneys that specialize in abusive business practices involving consumers.

Why is Date of Last Activity important?

This is important as a creditor might sell your account and the new owner of that debt might try to collect that debt. _What this does is reset the date of the negative item on your credit report._ This can be reported to the FTC as it violates the FCRA (Fair Credit Reporting Act), and this should encourage the new collector to remove the negative item

The FTC suggests using the following letter to dispute items on your credit report.

Date
Your Name
Your Address

Complaint Department
Name of Company
Address
City, State, Zip Code

Dear Sir or Madam:

I am writing to dispute the following information in my file. I have circled the items I dispute on the attached copy of the report I received.

This item (Name the item disputed such as creditors or tax court, and identify type of item which might be a credit account, judgment, etc.) is incorrect because (describe what is inaccurate or incomplete and why). I am requesting that the item be removed (or request another specific change) to correct the information.

Enclosed are copies of (describe any documentation attached to the letter, such as payment records and court documents) supporting my position. Please reinvestigate this matter and correct the disputed item as soon as possible.

Sincerely,
Your name

Rebuilding your credit after Debt Settlement

When starting out to rebuild your credit, here are a couple of things to keep in mind:

1. Get a secured credit card (the lender maintains a cash deposit that is equal to your credit limit) and use it very minimally. Usually it's easy to get a department store credit card, so try for that.
2. Make the payment on this card every month on time. Keep activity going on the card, proving that you are keeping your commitments in paying back what you owe. **DON'T run up a huge balance.**
3. Try not to apply for too much credit as the inquiries count against you.
4. Keep your debt to income ratio low.
5. Research some credit watch services like Experian Triple Advantage Monitoring
6. Use the piggyback method, which is to find a friend, or family member and get them to add you as an authorized user. This needs to be a reliable person who pays their own bills consistently, if not, it will affect your score.

You score should start improving when the accounts you have settled start showing on your report as zero.

Chapter 12: Life after Debt

....

Where do we go from here?

The purpose of this book is to help you settle the debt, but the staying out of debt after that is accomplished, will be up to you.

Methods to Staying out of Debt mean the following:

- Being adamantly determined not to spend on credit.
- **Cancelling all your credit cards** (yes, this is a tough one)
- Always having cash on you to pay for items.
- Using debit cards instead of credit cards
- Limiting yourself to buying items only when you've saved for them
- Creating a Budget and sticking to it.
- Finding cheaper places to buy groceries and clothing
- Starting a savings plan
- Finding new ways to make money – be innovative
- Create an emergency fund
- Create a holiday fund – this really is a great one especially if you've saved to figure out which cruise you're going to take, or which country you're going to visit
- Eat at home more
- Don't Sabotage yourself, and set yourself up for failure (Example "I'll just charge this and pay it off at the end of the month")
- Eliminate unnecessary items
- **Have a long term plan for wealth accumulation** with set goals for achievement and **feel good about having** lots of **money!**

Goal Setting:

The road to all good things is paved with goals. Be prepared to sit down and be brutally honest with how you are going to handle your future finances, how you will have savings and retirement set aside, as well as how you will handle your fun finances. One of the tried, proven and trusted ways is to set goals. There are many great books on goal setting, so I don't want to go through that in this book, but I would recommend you getting hold of a book or audio by Brian Tracy called "Goals!: How to Get Everything You Want" for a great breakdown on goal setting and achievement.

Fundamentals of Goal Setting are:

1. Make your goals specific and measurable.
2. Break the goals down in long term and short term goals.
3. Set dates by which each goal is to be achieved.
4. Share your goals with others, if that will help you stick to them.
5. Don't just have good intentions, put it in writing, and look at your goals frequently. Follow through!

Rainy day and fun money:

In the days when I was a freelance consultant making great money, the old rules my colleagues used to give me was to put aside six months of income for a rainy day, if you lost your job, or some emergency should happen. I know that this is kind of moot while facing the economy today, but, times will get better. Once you are debt-free focus on building up cash in the bank that is all yours. Have fun! Plan to give yourself rewards and great vacations. Most of all live, and enjoy your life. Some of us (yes I include myself) enjoyed life too much on credit cards. Now strive to live debt-free and pay cash for everything. It's a great thing to pay for a fun vacation from a pile of cash you have available.

I used to watch Suze Orman's financial advice on the television with frustration.

It was all about "do this, do that, and life will be great". Well it's not that easy to follow that kind of advice when you are badly in debt, and have lost your income, and are worried about the next mortgage payment. So in conclusion, stop worrying about your credit score for now, stash some cash, and start settling with the banks. The rest will all fall into place.

Chapter 13: Resource Section

………………..……………………………………………………

Additional resources for you

Please feel free to browse my website www.onlinedebtsettlement.info because I do constantly update that when any new relevant information is available. On the resource page of my website, it has direct link to some other of the resources not mentioned on this page.

IRS Publication 4681 – IRS Cancelled Debts, Foreclosures (Pub 4681)
http://www.irs.gov/pub/irs-pdf/p4681.pdf
IRS Publication 523 – Selling your home
http://www.irs.gov/pub/irs-pdf/p523.pdf

Federal Trade Commission
600 Pennsylvania Avenue, NW
Washington, DC 20580
877-382-4357
http://www.ftc.gov

Please check http://onlinedebtsettlement.info/Resources.html for additional links. This site is constantly being updated with any relevant debt settlement information, as well as the phone numbers of the banks for Short Sales, Loss Mitigation and Imminent Default.

There is also a page for all collection agencies. I have tried to put as many down as I can. If you know of one I've missed, please email ma and let me know.

Is this Morally Right?

It's very normal to feel guilty about not paying back what you owe. When feeling guilty, consider the following.

Let's say you owe $100,000 (round number again) with a 30% interest rate. Paying minimum payments, it would take you more than 50 years to pay that debt off. You need to pay $30,000 on that first year alone. What about principal? Let's say $5000, which would bring your principal balance to $95,000 How long would it take you to pay back what you originally borrowed? Paying the minimum payments starting at $3475 (This is interest plus 1% of the balance, using credit card calculator on Bankrate.com) it would take 608 months to pay it off with $255,647 in interest only. It's almost impossible to ever pay back the full debt. Now compare that to the $20,000 to $30,000 that you are going to settle your $100,000 debt by yourself for. So how much would you rather spend? **$355,000 (with the original principal) or $20,000 to $30,000?**

Month	Minimum Payment	Interest Paid	Principal Paid	Remaining Balance
1	$3,475.00	$2,500.00	$975.00	$99,025.00
2	$3,441.12	$2,475.62	$965.50	$98,059.88
607	$15.00	$0.45	$14.55	$3.42
608	$3.51	$0.09	$3.42	$0.00
Totals		255647.6	100001.5	

I hope that the answer to that will jump off the page to you. When you really look at the big picture of how much a credit card really costs you in the end, it's sickening. So, spend some time with the credit card calculators online (there are hundreds of them), and crunch the numbers.

Additional Information about Short Sales, Foreclosures and Loan Modifications

If you are having problems with overwhelming debt, the chances are, you are also having problems with your mortgage. Please check www.onlinedebtsettlement.info for helpful links, phone numbers and other resources for Foreclosures, Short Sales, Loan Modifications and other information available for these particular topics. There will also be an ongoing blog with questions and answers, and this website is constantly be added to.

There are many strategies available for homeowners struggling with overwhelming debt such as short sales, loan modifications, deed-in-lieu of foreclosure. All the **banks are now forced to offer these solutions** to struggling homeowners, although they take their time in doing so, and the progress is very slow. Federal regulations are now starting to enforce their compliance. When dealing with the banks about these issues, be thorough, document everything, ask for a name and ID number every time you call and speak to anyone. Check my website for updated phone numbers, and feel free to contribute any information you think might be helpful to others.

Some Tips for Loan Modifications:

1) Download the loan modification package from the bank's website.

2) At the top or bottom of each faxed page, put Borrower: Debbie Debtor and Loan Number: 123456789 (your loan information). It's also a good idea to number each page, so that they can identify which pages they are missing. Get all the information faxed to the bank, as soon as you can.

3) Follow up with the bank to see if they received your fax. If they say that they have not received your fax, fax again. Keep faxing over and over until they say the information has been received.

4) Call frequently even if they tell you not to. Don't allow several weeks to go by without contacting them, because they will come up with new documentation they need from you, and not tell you unless you diligently follow up. I recommend calling a minimum of twice a week.

5) Keep all your faxes and cover pages in a file.

6) When it does get assigned to a negotiator, follow up with that person often. Try to get the negotiator's email address. Sometimes it's easier to get people to respond by email than on the phone.

Utilizing the Office of the Comptroller of the Currency

If you get no response, write to the OCC (Office of the Comptroller of the Currency). The OCC supervises the national banks. They will open a file for you, and get attention to your case. Also "cc" the president of the bank.

Look at the following example of a letter (based on one I wrote to the OCC). They contacted the bank, and actually got my case moving. Even someone from the president's office at Chase contacted me. However, the end result of the modification did not suit me, and I ended up selling my home. Keep in mind this will work for Short Sales too.

Mandy Akridge
123 Mandy Street, Mandysville, CA 88888
555-551-5551

OCC - Office of the Comptroller of the Currency
Customer Assistance Group
1301 McKinney Street Suite 3450
Houston, Texas 77010-9050

Date: 10/7/2010

Dear Customer Assistance Group,

Re: Case 088584512362

Despite my efforts, as documented with your department with the case number above, to obtain a loan modification through Chase, I have once again been declined. This would make the **total number of declines three (each for different reasons).**

I applied with Chase back in December 2009, when I was current on the loan, indicating that hardship would be occurring within the next few months. I was declined then as well (after they lost the paperwork, was missing paperwork), my case was shut down, and I had to re-apply in May. After months of waiting, I was declined once again. Yesterday, I received a letter from Chase dated March 02, 2010 (please see attachment to this letter) stating I have been declined as the first mortgage is less that 31% of my gross income. I am unemployed and currently receive $xxx a month from Unemployment. So how could this be?

Here are the monthly numbers.

Income :

Unemployment	$1,000	
Possible other income loaned on temporary basis	$2,000	
Total		$3,000

Expenses:

Pick of 3 payments

Chase First Mortgage Negative Amortization:
> $2,900

Chase First Mortgage Interest Only:
> $3,400

Chase First Mortgage Full Principal and Interest:
> $4,400

Now, with my limited 12th grade math, taking $2900 (negative payment only) over $3000 I come up with 98.13%. My housing expense is 98.13% of my income (without including any other household expenses).

I would like an explanation from someone as to why I do not qualify for the Home Affordable Program. No-one from Chase contacted me to go over any numbers ever. Not even once during the three times I have applied for a modification. Also, I have a second mortgage of $xxx a month with Stupid mortgage Company, which I have not added into the equation above.

I believe I have been illegally declined for a loan modification by Chase and would like a lawyer representing me against this mortgage company, however, I am unable to currently afford one. Your help with this, or recommendations would be appreciated.

Your help is much appreciated, as it seems I have nowhere else to turn

Sincerely,
Mandy Akridge

Cc.

Jamie Dimon Chairman & Ceo Phone: 212-270-1111 Fax : 212-270-1121

David B. Lowman CEO Home Lending:

Phone: 636-735-2121 Fax: 314-256-2800

Chase Fulfillment Center: PO BOX 469030, Glendale, CO 80246-9030

United States Department of Housing and Urban Development
Office of RESPA and Interstate Land Sales
451 7th Street, SW, Room 9154
Washington, D.C. 20410

Some tips for Short Sales

If you are upside down on your home, and wish to sell by means of doing a short sale, here are some additional tips.

1) Find a realtor who specializes in short sales to help you.
2) The realtor needs to call the bank to request what necessary documentation is needed. Before they can talk to the bank on your behalf, they will need a letter of authorization from you.
3) The basic documentation needed by the bank will be a hardship letter, pay stubs, tax returns and bank statements. The quicker you get all the information to the banks, the faster your short sale will proceed.
4) Price your house very low, so that you will receive many offers. Don't have the highest offer submitted to the bank, otherwise, if your buyer walks away (and they often do, as the short sale process is extremely long), the bank won't be married to the high offer, and will be happy to accept other offers.
5) Make sure in your agreement with the realtor, that the lender pays all expenses, so nothing comes out of your own pocket. This is important wording and I would suggest having it included in your listing contract with the realtor, as well as noted on a counter offer to your prospective buyer.
6) When it does get assigned to a negotiator, follow up with that person often. Try to get the negotiator's email address. Sometimes it's easier

to get people to respond by email than on the phone.

7) Do not sign a promissory note for the remaining balance. Obtain a letter stating that the payment to the first and second lien holder satisfies the debt, and that you will not be pursued for the remaining balance. Absolutely insist on this wording, as you could find yourself being pursued legally after the sale of your home is complete. One thing to remember, if somehow you do get conned into signing a promissory note, it becomes an unsecured debt when your home is sold. Once it's unsecured, it works like any other credit card debt, absolutely negotiable.

8) Make sure all parties agree to the terms and payoff of the short sale. It's very important that all lien holders are on the same page.

9) Make sure the Mortgage holders put it in writing not to come after you for a deficiency.

Questions and Answers

Here are some questions and answers received from my online website and many emails received from readers who have read the book that might be useful to you.

Everyone is calling and offering me lower payments and reduced fees. All have been very polite and almost make me feel bad for doing this. I know you said they will get nastier as time goes by. I have to believe that in order to settle. Should I not agree to any of this?

I wouldn't, because then you're back where you started, still with big debt. Ultimately it's up to you. Wouldn't you rather not have debt?

If I stop paying all the credit cards, will the creditors will ask me to show them my hardship by providing them detailed financial statements including my pay check or assets?

No, the creditors won't ask you to send them anything. They will just keep calling you to ask for a payment

I am banking with Wells Fargo and I also have 1 credit card with Wells Fargo. I have some money in savings and checking accounts. If I stop paying my credit cards, and close the accounts with Wells Fargo, is Wells Fargo going to sue me or go after me if they think I am hiding the money?

I would make those accounts disappear quickly. Perhaps cash them out and keep your money as cash during this process. If you move it to another bank, it should be okay. The main thing is that you don't allow them to use the "Right of Offset" law, by having a checking account and a credit card account with the same bank.

My husband and I are both working, what kind of reason I can use to settle the debt? My husband lost his previous job 6 months ago

This is a great reason, as this set you very behind on your bills.

In the event that I cannot settle EVERY card, what will happen with the debt that I cannot settle? You said it will be considered a charge off. I know this will damage my credit. Will I be sued to pay this amount?

Not necessarily, the chances of being sued are low. The charge off only happens at around 180 days. I recommend trying to settle before then, as it is much less of a headache to deal with the original creditor, than the collection agencies.

I created a new bank account as you suggested and put all my money in there. I still have not closed down the other one, but there is only $5 in the account. My question is do I have to actually close down that account or can I just keep it dormant? I actually like banking with them and would like to use them again when everything is settled.

This one makes me laugh, because it's like borrowing $10 from your childhood friend, and telling him you're only going to pay him back $2, but is it okay if you still stay his friend? Remember, if they ever somehow get money for the settled account, even *after you settle, they are entitled to keep that money. You will see this stated in all the settlement letters that you receive from the bank.*

I just got off the phone with Citi Cards. I am 107 days late. I made a settlement offer that they declined. They said that on the 4th it would leave their pre-litigation department and then be transfer to a local attorney. I thought they charged off at 180 days. I am not sure what this all means or the next step to do. We just cannot make their offer. I am not sure if this is one of the scare tack ticks they use.

I think they are just trying to scare you. It's unlikely it's charged off yet. I would wait and see, and keep gently suggesting a settlement, maybe once a week or every two weeks. Take note of where the "attorney" is located. If it's not in your town, it is more than likely an attorney firm acting as a collection agency.

For the 6 months that I am not paying my bills, the interest and total debt is accumulating. When it comes time to settle, will they settle on the amount I owe now or the total amount that is owed at the end of six months? In other words, what I am saying is should I plan on saving a whole lot more to settle with, since the total amount I am going to owe at the end of 6 months will be much greater than what I owe now?

Yes ,the amount you owe after 6 months will be more, but it won't work out to be that much more when you consider you'll be settling for 20 -30 cents to the dollar.

I have a credit card account with Chase and also my auto loan through them. I'm obviously going to stop the auto pay on the Chase credit card but would prefer to keep my auto loan on auto pay. Is that a bad idea since it's through the same company?

I wouldn't particularly encourage you to leave anything on autopay while you are going through this process with Chase. The right of offset applies to when you have a checking account and a credit account in the same bank, and the banks have hinted that they have affiliations with other banks and might be able to reach into there. I don't believe that, and have not experienced it, and had credit cards with all the major banks. You need to be more concerned if your account has been charged off and handed to a collection agency. Those are the ones who will try to find any assets you may have.

I recently purchased your book "Negotiate and Settle Your Debts- A Debt Settlement Strategy" excellent source of information. I know every situation is different but I wanted to see if you had any inside information when dealing with Capital One. I am currently almost 180 days behind and I called then asking if they would accept a settlement. They told me that they would however the amount was like 75 cents on the dollar.

It looks like you might need to let them send this to collections to get a better settlement. Capital 1is notoriously tough. Keep offering settlements and stick to your story. There are people out there getting decent enough settlements.

Thank you so much for giving your time to help those of us in need. We went into the settlement process because we just have too many bills for too little a paycheck. My question is...do I HAVE to give out how much my husband makes and what our mortgage payment, car payment, bills are? Someone from Chase wanted that information, as well as someone from United Recovery Systems (which my AE card went to after only 90days late). :(I am trying not to get rattled as I am so close...almost ALL of our 8 cards that we let go are past 90 days.

You don't have to give out any personal information. It is none of their business; they are just trying to get hold of your bank account information, and other personal details, so they can determine if you can pay. Just keep to your hardship story, and when the time is right, offer settlements. Check to see who owns the collection agency, as it might be the original creditor.

I'm on day 88 with AMEX. I spoke with them today and she asked if I have any savings and I said "no. She immediately said that since I have no battle plan, she is going to recommend that they sell this to a third party and that I should hear from them in a couple of weeks. Do you think she is bluffing? Should I call them back and let them know that I might be able to look at a 401k or something like that?

I would wait and see, It's still very early days. Why not see what their next move is. In another month, it will be four months, and then you could bring up settlement again. When you do bring up the subject of settling, make sure to tell them you can obtain the funds from a family member, relative..etc.

In Closing

In conclusion, I do receive many emails from people who purchased my book. I do try to answer everyone, but unfortunately it is becoming harder to keep track of as the numbers of emails are increasing. At this stage, my email is still up for you to ask any questions, but it may not be in the future.

Should you have any questions, please feel free to email me at debtsettler@ymail.com

I do not claim to be an "expert" but am happy to answer questions from within my realm of experience. The feeling of getting your final settlements achieved is so great, when you have those letters in hand, that you want to go out and celebrate with Champagne and click your heels together. I sincerely hope that you get to experience that, and would love to hear your success stories.

My goal is to make the website www.onlinedebtsettlement.info a valuable resource to all those out there struggling with overwhelming debt, and value any contributions from you. Let's help each other get out of debt, one credit card at a time.

Good Luck to you, and go and settle those debts to move on to a debt free joyous life! Once you get out of debt, do your best to stay out of debt. Determine to never use credit cards again unless absolutely necessary!

THE END

Made in the USA
Lexington, KY
08 December 2011